# Catholic Perspectives on Peace and War

Thomas J. Massaro, S.J.
and
Thomas A. Shannon

A SHEED & WARD BOOK

ROWMAN & LITTLEFIELD PUBLISHERS, INC.
*Lanham • Boulder • New York • Toronto • Oxford*

A SHEED & WARD BOOK

ROWMAN & LITTLEFIELD PUBLISHERS, INC.

Published in the United States of America
by Rowman & Littlefield Publishers, Inc.
A wholly owned subsidary of The Rowman & Littlefield Publishing Group, Inc.
4501 Forbes Boulevard, Suite 200, Lanham, Maryland 20706
www.rowmanlittlefield.com

PO Box 317
Oxford
OX2 9RU, UK

British Library Cataloguing in Publication Information Available

**Library of Congress Cataloging-in-Publication Data**

Massaro, Thomas, 1961–
    Catholic perspectives on peace and war / Thomas J. Massaro and
Thomas A. Shannon.
        p. cm.
    Includes bibliographical references and index.
    ISBN 0-7425-3175-9 (alk. paper)—ISBN 0-7425-3176-7 (pbk. : alk. paper)
    1. Peace—Religious aspects—Catholic Church. 2. War—Religious aspects—
Catholic Church. I. Shannon, Thomas A. (Thomas Anthony), 1940– II. Title.

BX1795.P43M27 2003
241'.6242—dc21                                                          2003013759

Printed in the United States of America

∞ ™ The paper used in this publication meets the minimum requirements of
American National Standard for Information Sciences—Permanence of Paper
for Printed Library Materials, ANSI/NISO Z39.48-1992.

Thomas J. Massaro dedicates this work to his five nieces and three nephews. May they grow up in a peaceful world, one free of the scourge of war.

Thomas A. Shannon dedicates this work to his dear daughters Ashley and Courtney and his new son-in-law Dino. I wish all of you the gift of peace.

# Contents

# Preface

Hammer your ploughshares into swords, your sickles into spears.

Joel 4:10

These will hammer their swords into ploughshares, their spears into sickles.

Isaiah 2:4

The biblical ambivalence and paradox exemplified above indicates only a small part of the dilemmas one encounters in trying to establish an ethical analysis of war. The contemporary tension was set out clearly by Pope John Paul II in his 1982 World Day of Peace message:

> This is why Christians, even as they strive to resist and prevent every form of warfare, have no hesitation in recalling that, in the name of an elementary requirement of justice, peoples have a right and even a duty to protect their existence and freedom by proportionate means against an unjust aggressor. . . . In view of the difference between classical warfare and nuclear or bacteriological wars—a difference so to speak of nature—and in view of the scandal of the arms race seen against the background of the needs of the third world, this right, which is very real in principle, only underlines the urgency for world society to equip itself with effective means of negotiation.

The tension between the right to self-defense and the dramatically changed nature of war constitutes the context in which the moral concerns about war are set forth. While we are concerned with the history of the just war theory, we are also concerned with the moral arguments about war that emerge out of the American context, especially at this time after both terrorist attacks and the possible use of weapons of mass destruction. A tremendous change is occurring in the moral analysis of war, particularly in light of the reality of terrorist attacks, and we wish to reflect on that development in particular through the lens offered by the U.S. Bishops in their most extensive treatment of the ethics of military action in the 1983 pastor letter *The Challenge of Peace*.

We hope that this presentation will illuminate many of the issues that are involved in the current discussion of the ethics of warfare and terrorism and that it will make a contribution to the development of an American Catholic moral analysis of war.

# 1

✛

# The Development of
# the Just War Tradition

## WAR AND ANCIENT CULTURES AND RELIGIONS

It is a fact of history and of life that violence and war seem to have always been with us. From a biological point of view, species have always competed, with one species using another for its food supply. This helps preserve the chain of life and, consequently, maintains population stability and ecological balance. What is unique about human behavior is that, in stark contrast to the majority of animal species, humans kill each other, sometimes to gain food and land but also for ideological reasons. This reality is highlighted most starkly in our contemporary world. While other animals certainly battle to maintain territorial and sexual status, these ritual battles do not always result in the death of the opponents. Our routine killing of members of our own species stands in sharp contrast to that behavior. For better or worse, human beings seem to be unique, not only with respect to consciousness and language abilities, but also for their ability to engage in killing of their own kind.

In spite of this ongoing violence of our species, almost every culture and civilization postulated some type of golden age in which all peoples lived in harmony. This hypothesized age came in a variety of forms but the basic belief was fairly constant: once upon a time, people lived in peace, shared what they had, and life was harmonious. Whether this golden age is a dim memory from the origins of our race, or whether it is simply an expression of deep longing of human beings, such an age was not a reality, at least not for any civilizations that we know. It is certainly not the case at the present time. And for better or worse, most religions of

1

the ancient world, as well as contemporary religions, have found a way to justify or accommodate themselves to the reality of war.[1] The following is a brief survey of the teachings about war according to the ancient religions and cultures.

## Hinduism

Hinduism, the traditional religion of India, is among the most ancient of the world religions. One of its unique features is that it defined a specific warrior caste. The members of this caste had to live out their *dharma* (fate) by doing what was appropriate for their particular state in life. The military duties defined by membership in this caste transcended family obligations, and fidelity to them ensured a favorable outcome to one's destiny.

Hinduism, however, provided rules for the conduct of war. Members of a cavalry unit would fight only against other cavalry units, and infantry could fight only against other infantry. In a foreshadowing of later theories of war, Hinduism mandated that the wounded, prisoners, runaways, and other noncombatants be treated in a respectful manner.

Hinduism did not allow all members of the religion to fight; it relegated that duty to one specific caste and assigned specific rules for the conduct of how war was to be carried out.

## Jainism

The one major exception to the sanctioning of war and killing by the ancient religions and cultures is that of Jainism. Jainism is an offshoot of Hinduism and has continued to exist in a relatively pure form to the present day. Jainism focused on the doctrine of *ahimsa*: a renunciation of the will or desire to kill or harm any living organism. This was carried to its logical conclusion so that Jains were recognized by the gauze masks they wore over their mouths lest they accidentally breathe in and swallow an insect; by their habit of sweeping the ground before them with a broom so that they would not step on any organism; and, in particular, by a steadfast refusal to kill any living being. Jains typically withdrew from the world, ate food prepared by others and obtained through begging, refused to practice agriculture, and would not engage in any type of violent activities. In a world of growing violence, the Jains were conspicuous by their nonviolence and what could be characterized as a type of pacifism. Their vision provided the inspiration for Gandhi's philosophy of nonviolence. While many people argued that the Jains are irrelevant because of their lifestyle, they have at least had a significant impact on civilization through inspiring a whole philosophy of nonviolence.

## Buddhism

The ancient religion of Buddhism, predominant in some areas of India, Japan, and China, had as the first of its five major precepts a prohibition on killing. This obligation was binding upon both the monks and the laity. For killing to be considered a sin, several conditions had to be simultaneously met: the one killed had to be, in fact, a living being; the person doing the killing had to know that this individual was a living being; there had to be an intent to kill; appropriate means had to be used (these included bare hands, orders given to others, the use of weapons or other instruments, trapping, magic, or the forces of one's mind); and, finally, death had to actually occur. While these rules could be used in a casuistic fashion to justify some forms of killing as not being morally reprehensible, they indicate nonetheless the seriousness with which the precept was taken and its significance within the religion.

Mahayana Buddhism, a liberal form of Buddhism that developed approximately a century after the death of the Buddha, allowed several justifications for killing. Some of these have a very ironic modern ring to them. Killing was allowed to protect the purity of Buddhist doctrine. In an extreme situation, it was morally preferable to kill one person rather than have two individuals die. Finally, Mahayana Buddhism postulated that it was better to kill another person rather than to allow that person to kill someone else.

Thus, although there is in Buddhism a strong emphasis on not killing, openings began to be made, and these provided the basis for an expansion of the justifications for killing.

## Greece and Rome

In these two ancient civilizations, peace was prized—in Greece as a state of order and coherence and in Rome as an agreement between parties not to fight. Nonetheless, both of these cultures were continuously and deeply involved in the enterprise of war. Although seen by the Stoic philosophers as irrational and contrary to the structure of the universe, war was frequently waged nonetheless, oftentimes to gain the harvest of the neighboring town or city or to conquer the known world. This was the case with Alexander the Great, who picked up where his father, Philip II of Macedon, left off. Rome also fought to extend its rule over the known world, although it attempted to do this through concessions and negotiations as well as conquests. In both cultures there were gods and goddesses of peace as well as of war. The army was perceived to be for waging war as well as a police force for ensuring domestic harmony.

Both of these empires relied on their armies to ensure their rule throughout the known world, and then they relied on them to maintain the order that they had secured. Peace was prized, but war was important and quite frequently the means to achieve the goal of peace. The legacy of Rome at the beginning of Christianity was the *Pax Romana*, but this was a peace forged through the waging of war and enforced through a standing army.

## Judaism

As a religion, Judaism was born in a slave rebellion, and after the Exodus from Egypt the Israelites wandered for years in the desert. Eventually the nation was established through a gradual process of the conquest of the Canaanites, the people who occupied what was to become the ancient nation of Israel. Thus, one dimension of Judaism, especially reflected in many of its Scriptures, justified war and various battles as a way of fulfilling the mandate that Yahweh had given them to establish their own land. In many of these passages, God is defined as a warrior and as one who directs battles and ensures victory.

Yet there is another strand in Judaism in which the ideal of peace is presented. Many of these passages are found in the writings of prophets in which there is a looking forward to the messianic age when all of God's promises will be fulfilled and an age of peace will be established.

The rabbinic tradition distinguished two types of war: optional war and obligatory war. An optional war is basically a defensive war in which a nation initiates a preemptive strike to avoid being attacked. The tradition did not easily justify this type of war and it was always suspect. The obligatory war was in response to an attack from the outside. The purpose of war here was to defend oneself, to protect one's home and homeland. Yet, even in this mandated war of defense, there were limits. Fruit trees, fields, and homes could not be destroyed. Women, especially those taken prisoner, were to be treated humanely. And the Jewish army could lay siege to a town only on three sides so that those who wished to escape could do so.

The Jewish tradition affirms the desirability of peace but also recognizes, especially in its historical circumstances, the necessity of war. While the tradition affirms the significance of peace and its desirability and eventual presence in the messianic kingdom, it also affirms the right of the people to defend themselves by repelling an enemy. Even here, however, the tradition recognizes that there must be limits in how one does this and in this way seeks to establish the seeds of peace even while fighting continues.

## Zoroastrianism

A Mideastern religion popular around the sixth century before our common era, Zoroastrianism used military metaphors to describe its main theological insight: life was a battle between the forces of light and the forces of darkness. This religion postulated an eschatological battle in which the forces of good would eventually triumph, and it also provided the ideological background for the growing nationalism under way in the ancient Persian Empire. Zoroastrianism provided both a basis for ideological unity as well as the inspiration for the many and frequent wars that were fought during the expansion of the empire.

For the Zoroastrians, life was seen as a battle and, not unsurprisingly, this religion provided a basis for many of the polemics during the formation and expansion of the Persian Empire.

## Islam

One of the central concepts of Islam, the youngest of the major world religions, is that of the Jihad: a striving in the way of God, or a pursuit of the worship of God. The Jihad is the way in which the member of Islam lives out the obligation to submit totally to the rule of God in one's life. For some adherents to Islam, there is a military dimension to the Jihad as well. One version sees Jihad in the narrow sense as a war of self-defense against a non-Islamic invader. Others with a more expansive view of Jihad argue that it is appropriate to extend the rule of Islam through military means or to go to war against unbelievers or enemies of the faith. In this military sense, then, the Jihad is a justified religious war fought against polytheists, apostates, or some enemy of Islam. Its major purpose is to establish a universal theocratic state bound together in the worship of Allah, the one true God. The concept of the Jihad in Islam is in many ways analogous to the concept of the crusade that we encounter in Christianity. It is a holy war fought against a religious enemy to establish the rule of God over all peoples.

As in the other religions we have discussed, rules exist in Islam for the conduct of war. Primary among these is the rule that noncombatants are to be spared unless they are indirectly helping the cause of the enemy. The areas that can be destroyed are limited to those that cannot be brought under the political or military control of Islam. Also, animals are to be spared, although crops and inanimate objects can be destroyed. Interestingly enough in a desert country, the water supply can be destroyed or poisoned.

Also, as in other religions, there are different religious divisions in Islam as well as reform movements. One such movement derives from a medieval school of Arabic thought known as Salafiyya. This movement, now revived in the twentieth century, shifted from a position of a rapprochement with Western ideas to the position that contemporary Western culture is corrupt and mirrors the infidelity of the world prior to the revelation of Islam. This movement also justified the overthrow of a Muslim government by other Muslims by arguing that their faithlessness to traditional practices reduced them to the state of infidels and that they were, therefore, unfit to rule a Muslim country. Another movement is Wahhabism, named after Abd al-Wahhab, an early nineteenth-century Saudi Arabian scholar who also saw in the religious decline of his country the idolatrous conditions that mirrored the situation at the time of Muhammad. The solution was a return to a strict interpretation of the Quran and the ethics and mores of the community at Medina in the seventh century. Currently, this movement is partly responsible for the tension in Saudi Arabia between critics of modernity and relations with the West and those critics of the current leadership and the lifestyle of the royal family. These two particular movements have helped structure perceptions of and relations with the West in terms of a self-sufficient and reformed Islam, thus making such relations much more difficult. Life in the United States, in particular, is seen as contrary to Islamic values and beliefs, and this perception, when joined with other ideological claims, makes misunderstanding and perhaps conflict a natural outcome.

## CHRISTIANITY

Like other major world religions, Christianity developed a position on war. The remaining sections of this chapter will sketch out different dimensions of this development.[2]

### The Early Community

Christianity began its development as a sect of Judaism. The early Christians maintained strong ties with the Jewish community and, in fact, continued to participate actively in Judaism. Only after the growing realization of the significance of the claim that Jesus was the Son of God did the split between the Christian and Jewish communities begin to grow. Over the course of several decades, differences in theology, worship, and community organization helped the Christians develop their own autonomy and distinctiveness from Judaism.

Like many other peoples during this particular time period of history, the Christians were awaiting the end of the world. The specific content of this hope was focused around the imminent return of the resurrected and glorified Jesus. The early Christians assumed that Jesus would return, if not within their lifetime, certainly within the lifetime of their children. The first Christian community lived its life in the expectation that at any moment God's kingdom would break into their world and bring it and them to their fulfillment with God.

Because of this, the earliest Christians tended not to become involved in the life and structures of the community around them. Since they were awaiting the imminent return of Jesus, the needs of everyday life as well as the significance of social institutions took on less and less importance to them. While such an attitude may be difficult for us to understand in our present situation, nonetheless such an expectation of the imminent end of the world goes a long way toward explaining why Christians focused on celibacy, why they did not participate in government and education, and why, often enough, they even quit their jobs. The extent of this withdrawal from the world can be seen in Paul's Second Letter to the Thessalonians in which he chides the Christian community and requests that they return to work instead of sitting around waiting for the world to end. In 2 Thessalonians 3:10, for example, Paul rather directly says that those who do not work should not eat.

Christians were typically not involved in the affairs of the larger community around them. The early members of the Christian community were drawn from the lower socioeconomic classes, and their marginal status helps explain why many more of them were not actively involved in the affairs of the empire. But more importantly, the early community perceived no religious social mandate to change the obvious inequities of the society around them. Without motivation to change what they saw, and seduced by their expectation of the end of the world, the Christians saw no gain in entering the structures of the world around them.

## The Changing Situation

As a matter of very obvious fact, the world did not end within the first generation of the founding of Christianity. The delay of the second coming of Jesus constituted the first major crisis of faith within the early community. This crisis was resolved by affirming that Jesus would indeed return and bring the world to its heavenly consummation—but that this would be at an unknown future time. Such an explanation was based on interpretations of some of the different parables, for example, the one in which the Son of Man is described as coming like a thief in the night and at a time when the homeowner is not on guard.

This delay meant that if Christians were to survive personally and socially, they could no longer remain exclusively within the confines of their community. And indeed, once they realized that the world was not going to end, Christians began to participate more and more in the affairs of the community around them. This turning outward on the part of the Christian community was also enhanced and somewhat necessitated because of the growth of the community and because of the presence of Christians in different socioeconomic strata within the empire.

The continuation of the world, a growing community, and a much more economically mixed community brought about pressures for the Church to develop an ethic that would take this changed social situation into account. Once the faces of Christians were turned outward to the world instead of being focused primarily on the heavens looking for the return of Jesus, they had to take into account the conditions in which they lived to determine how one might live as a Christian within the world. One important area of this development of a new Christian social ethic had to do with examining the reality of war.

## THE DEVELOPMENT OF THE JUST WAR THEORY

### The Tradition of the Early Church

"From the end of the New Testament period to the decade A.D. 170–180 there is no evidence whatever of Christians in the army."[3] This claim by Roland Bainton is fairly well accepted. The problem is in trying to explain why this was the case. One explanation undoubtedly has to do with Christians' not typically joining in the structures of the larger society. Another reason is the slow growth of Christianity among those classes who were likely to be soldiers. Also, soldiers had to participate in the religious services of the empire, behavior that was considered idolatry by Christians. Finally, the Church had a rigorist morality that uneasily readmitted to Communion people who committed apostasy, adultery, or bloodshed. The Christians were attempting to live out the love ethic of Jesus, and such an ethic would, at least *prima facie*, rule out the shedding of blood.

### Participation in the Army and War

The year 180 marks the turning point for participation of Christians in the military. Christians showed up in one of Marcus Aurelius's legions. Tertullian provides indirect evidence of the presence of Christians in the palace, the senate, the forum, and the army. During the persecution of Decius in 250, there is a reference to soldier martyrs. In 303, Galerius tried to eliminate Christians from his army. Service in the army was legitimated because it also served as a type of police force. Finally, Christians seemed more likely to participate in war the closer they were to the frontiers of the empire, assumedly because of the perceived danger to the nation.

These developments reflect a tension in the early Christian attitude toward war. On the one hand, there was a recognition that killing was, if not incompatible with Christianity, at least very difficult to justify. On the other hand, there was a growing practice of Christians serving in the army. At times it was easy to argue against service to the empire by being a soldier because of the necessity of participating in idolatry through taking the required oath of allegiance that affirmed Caesar as a god or because the Roman army was the instrument through which the empire persecuted Christians. If love were the supreme value for Christians, then fighting and killing were difficult to justify. On the other hand though, as Christianity grew, soldiers also converted and there is no record of any requirement to resign. As the expectation of Jesus' imminent return began to lessen, Christians naturally gravitated toward available ways of making a living, and the army provided one of these. Then too, especially on the edges of the empire, there was a need to defend the empire against the incursions of the barbarians. Finally, the more the army took on the function of a police force, the less problematic service in that army became.

Two external forces changed the early Church's tilt toward pacifism or nonviolence. The first was the unification of the Roman Empire under Constantine, one dimension of which was his establishing Christianity as the official religion of the Roman Empire. In addition to having one faith, one Lord, and one baptism there was now one empire and one emperor. Such a situation allowed a significant assimilation of Christians into all dimensions of the life of the empire. Additionally, Christianity now had a privileged position as the religion of the empire—a dramatic reversal from the persecutions only so recently experienced.

The second factor responsible for the change in orientation of Christianity toward war came as a result of the growing invasions of the so-called barbarians. The issue here, simply stated, was that since Christianity was now the religion of the empire, its survival was intimately bound up with the fate of the empire. If Christianity were to survive, so must the empire. Therefore, when the fate of the empire was in jeopardy, it was appropriate to defend the empire so that Christianity might survive.

## THE ETHICAL JUSTIFICATION OF WAR IN CHRISTIANITY

### St. Ambrose (339–397)

The first major ethic of war came from Ambrose. Before being elected to the bishopric of Milan, Ambrose had been the Pretorian Prefect of northern Italy. He was thus no stranger to the army and to the purposes it could fulfill. These purposes became more apparent to him because of the invasion of the barbarians, who presented the additional danger of being the bearers of various heresies, such as Arianism. By developing an ethic justifying war, the empire's boundaries could be maintained and even expanded and doctrinal purity could be enforced and new converts made.

Ambrose developed his Christian ethic of war from two sources. The first of these used the many military examples from the Jewish Scriptures adopted by the Christians. The campaigns conducted by the Jewish people in the conquest of the land of Canaan provided many examples that helped to justify Christian participation in war. Second, Ambrose adopted a Stoic ethic through his own study of Cicero, especially the work *De Officiis*, in which Cicero developed a type of just war theory. Briefly stated, Cicero argued that the only justified cause of going to war was that we might live unharmed in a time of peace. When the victory was won, mercy should be shown to those who had lost. Also, no war should be entered unless there had been an official demand for satisfaction given or a formal declaration made, following an appropriate warning. War could be entered to preserve the safety of a city, to protect the innocent, to avenge wrongs, and to honor pledges made to allies.

Ambrose adopted these elements for his theory of a just war, but he argued that clerics should not participate in war. The image of clerics fighting in war seemed to be incompatible with the duty of their office, which focused primarily on duties to the soul as well as on a ministry of reconciliation.

## Augustine (354–430)

The major thrust for the full development of a Christian ethic of war came from Augustine, one of the most influential of all Catholic theologians. Augustine's context is important in understanding his orientation toward war. Though born in Africa, Augustine was a classically trained Roman philosopher, familiar with the writings of the best philosophers of his age. He was also a longtime and deeply committed member of the Manichean religion, and much of his later life was spent in repenting these teachings. Finally, Augustine was instructed in Catholicism by Ambrose, a member of a mature Catholicism, one that was co-extensive with the empire and that now had a relatively clear tradition of its own, as well as a recognized center in Rome. In his years as Bishop of Hippo, Augustine lived in North Africa, and this province of the Roman Empire was in danger of being invaded by the Vandals. Only the Roman army stood between them and the destruction of the empire. All of these elements combined to persuade Augustine that order and the empire were preferable to chaos and that the survival of Christianity was tied up with the fate of the empire. Because the empire was Christian, the Church might be able to give some guidance and achieve some measure of justice. Therefore the empire could be defended and Christians could participate in that defense.

In his major work on political order, *The City of God*, Augustine said, "A just war, moreover, is justified only by the injustice of an aggressor, and that injustice ought to be a source of grief to any good man, because it is human injustice."[4] This serves as the primary justification for declaring war and participating in it. Eventually in his other writings, Augustine added on other dimensions that were to serve as the framework for the development of the just war theory in Catholicism: war was to be waged only under the authority of the ruler; the conduct of the war must be just; and, as he learned from Ambrose, the clergy could not participate in war.

Augustine was not looking for the possibility of Christian perfection on earth. He recognized that injustice and war would be part of the reality of life in his age. On the other hand, he felt that Christianity should try to humanize war as much as possible. He regarded peace as an ideal and tried to make the rules of war conducive to this end. In trying to restrain war, Augustine hoped that justice could be restored and that love could continue to be the dominant disposition that would rule the relationship between individuals. For Augustine, however, love was an interior attitude or disposition compatible with various actions, including killing an enemy out of the motive of love. Realism had entered Christianity.

### Thomas Aquinas (1225–1274)

Because of the quality of his theological reflections and his status within the theological community, the thought of Aquinas played a most significant role in the development of traditional Roman Catholic theology. In his major work, the *Summa Theologica*, Aquinas elucidates his teachings on war. Thomas Gilby offers this summary:

> There are three conditions of a just war. First, war is to be waged only under the authority and command of the sovereign. It is not the business of the private citizen to declare war or to summon the nation to arms. The second condition is that the hostility of war is a response to some crime on the part of the enemy. Therefore Augustine observes that a just war is one that avenges wrongs, i.e., a nation or state has to be punished for refusing to make amends for the injuries done by its people or to restore what has been seized unjustly. The third condition is a rightful intention, the advancement of good or the avoidance of evil. It may happen that a war declared by a legitimate authority for a just cause may yet be rendered unlawful through a wicked intention. And Aquinas declares that the passion for inflicting harm, the cruel thirst for vengeance, a plundering and implacable spirit, the fever of turmoil, or the lust for power and suchlike, all these are justly condemned in war.[5]

Aquinas also prohibited bishops and clergy from participating in war because their ministry was directed to the service of God. Thus, as in Augustine's thought, the clergy were held to the norm of pacifism and could not rely on worldly weapons for their own defense.

## SUMMARY

By the end of the thirteenth century, the major elements of the Christian
ethic of war were in place. The Church had moved from a position of non-
involvement and nonviolence and perhaps even pacifism to a situation of
significant involvement within the Roman Empire and society at large.
This new situation included the possibility of engaging in the defense of
that society. This was done partly out of a sense that the empire was worth
defending as a means of preserving the empire and Christianity with it,
and partly out of the sense that the Church could help to humanize the reality of war by making it a rule-governed activity. The basic criteria for
conducting a just war at this period can be summarized as follows: war
must be declared by the authority of the state; there must be a just cause;
the intention must be just; war must be the last resort; only right means
may be employed in the conduct of war; there must be a reasonable hope
of victory; and the good to be achieved must outweigh the evils of war.

Christians were now to find themselves in a variety of situations in
which they were able to participate in fighting. These ranged from the defense of the empire against the barbarians to the participation in the Crusades fought at the instigation of the Church and state, both to repel the
Muslims from the Roman Empire and to try to impose Christianity on
them. Such crusades would be replicated in the West in the various wars
of religion that would devastate Christianity and Europe following the
Reformation.

The tradition of the just war was also complemented by the assumption
that citizens were basically to obey the command of the state, even a command to participate in war. This tradition and some of the motivations and
justifications for it are exemplified nicely in the quote from the sixteenth-
century Spanish moral theologian Francisco de Vitoria.

> Other lesser folk who have no place or audience in the prince's counsel or in
> the public counsel are under no obligation to examine the causes of war but
> may serve in it in reliance on their betters. This is proved, first, by the fact
> that it is impossible and inexpedient to give reasons for all kinds of acts of
> state to every member of the commonalty. Also by the fact that men of the
> lower orders, even if they perceived the injustice of a war, could not stop it,
> and their voice would not be heeded. Therefore, any examination by them of
> the causes of a war would be futile. Also by the fact that for men of this sort
> it is enough proof of the justice of war (unless the contrary be quite certain)
> that it is being waged after public counsel and by public authority. Therefore
> no further examination on their part is needed.[6]

The tradition of having Christians participate in war became well established. The just war became the dominant ethic with respect to war.

The alternative of pacifism was perceived to be a counsel of the gospel and was not obligatory, and in fact, it often was perceived to be an inappropriate response when the state was in danger. Of course pacifism was expected of the clergy and of members of religious orders. Thus, while pacifism remained a modest option, the dominant and received tradition is that of sanctioning the participation of Christians in war.

# 2

✝

# Survey of Roman Catholic Teachings on War and Peace

## THE EARLY CHURCH

As indicated in the previous chapter, the primary attention of the early Church was on its own spiritual development while awaiting the return of Jesus. Nonetheless as time passed and the world did not end—nor did it appear likely to do so—the Church became involved in the affairs of the world. The Church was also increasing in members, many of whom were from a broader socioeconomic background. Yet the Church's full assimilation into the Roman Empire was slowed by persecutions based on two different, but related, perceptions. First, Christians threatened the stability of the empire because they would not participate in emperor worship. Second, the Roman authorities felt that this new religion could create political threats by providing an alternative ideological perspective that would disrupt the unity of the empire. Nonetheless, even in spite of serious persecutions, the Church continued to grow. When Constantine became the emperor early in the fourth century, Christianity became the official state religion of the Roman Empire, and members of the Church, including the hierarchy, took an even more active role in the affairs of state.

The contributions of Ambrose and Augustine to the development of justifications for a Christian's participation in war have already been mentioned. Yet both of these individuals should be remembered for their repeated efforts to achieve peace. Ambrose, for example, demanded that Emperor Theodosius (346–395) perform public penance for a massacre of the inhabitants of Thessalonica in 390. Augustine, too, made numerous appeals for peace and for clemency to help resolve the aftermath of the many wars that he witnessed.

A new role was played by the popes of this era. Pope Innocent I (402–417) served as a mediator between the Roman Empire and the Visigothic King Alaric I. Pope Leo I (440–461) continued this role by his appeal to the fifth century Hun warlord Attila. Leo attempted to mediate again when Genseric, king of the land-hungry Vandals, led another invasion of the empire. Although not as successful as he was with Attila, Leo was able to restrain some of the excesses of the invasion. Gregory I (590–604) established some communication with the invading Lombards, a Germanic people bent on moving south into Italy, and helped maintain order within the struggling empire. Unfortunately, for several centuries after Gregory, the popes became embroiled in local politics and focused on their own political interests. Consequently, they were unable to serve as mediators.

In the year 910, the Abbey of Cluny was founded in eastern France and began to help reform the religious and civil life of Europe. The abbot of Cluny was responsible for helping to initiate the Peace of God, a juridical code of behavior, the major intent of which was to exempt certain classes of persons from the operations of war and to mark off a sphere of peace. Noncombatants, defenseless people, and members of the clergy were declared immune from attack under these conventions.

The Cluniac reforms were succeeded in the eleventh century by the Truce of God, a more developed code that restrained wars by restricting the times when combat could occur. One truce prohibited fighting from Wednesday vespers to sunrise on Monday. Other truces prohibited fighting during specific liturgical seasons: from the beginning of Advent to the octave of the Epiphany, from the beginning of Easter to its octave, and from the first of the Rogation days to the octave of Pentecost. While not eliminating war or reducing the amount of violence that occurred during a war, both the Peace of God and the Truce of God, when strictly enforced, did at least restrict the time when fighting could occur and served as a check on the violence at that time. Pope Urban II (1088–1099), at the Council of Clermont, attempted to reintroduce the Truce of God and declare anathema those who broke it voluntarily. In the council of Rheims in 1119, the Truce was reenacted and the Second Lateran Council, an important ecumenical council held in 1139, put the final touches on its institutionalization. The Third Lateran Council, in 1179, made the Truce universal law for the entire Church by incorporating parts of it into canon law. This, of course, did not guarantee its observance, and eventually the Truce of God became part of the history of the Church rather than its active teaching.

Another very important limitation on war came through the preaching of the mendicant orders, especially the Franciscans. In addition to his own personal efforts to reduce violence in the Crusades, St. Francis's rule for the Third Order prohibited members from carrying weapons on their person. This was a significant blow to warfare during feudal times and, in fact, helped reduce war qualitatively and quantitatively.

## THE MEDIEVAL CHURCH

During the Middle Ages, the Church achieved a remarkable theological, philosophical, and cultural integration. In part this was due to the growing unity of the Roman Empire and in part to the presence of a number of gifted individuals such as the founders of the mendicant orders, several brilliant theologians such as Aquinas and Bonaventure (1221–1274), and an extremely gifted Pope, Innocent III (1160–1216). During this time the theory of the just war reached a point of major synthesis in the systematic development of Catholic theology. As already mentioned, Aquinas put the insights of Ambrose and Augustine into a more structured form. The late Scholastic theologians Francisco de Vitoria (1486–1546) and Francisco Suárez (1548–1617) continued to develop the insights of Aquinas.

Vitoria, in his *De Jure Belli*, summarized the three rules of war as follows:

First Canon: Assuming that a prince has authority to make war, he should first of all not go seeking occasions and causes of war, but should, if possible, live in peace with all men as St. Paul enjoins on us.

Second Canon: When war for a just cause has broken out it must not be waged so as to ruin the people to whom it is directed, but only so as to obtain one's rights and the defense of one's country and in order that from that war peace and security may in time result.

Third Canon: When victory has been won, victory should be utilized with moderation and Christian humility, and the victor ought to deem that he is sitting as judge between two states, the one which has been wronged and the one which has done the wrong, so that it will be as judge and not as accuser that he will deliver the judgment whereby the injured state can obtain satisfaction, and this, so far as possible, should involve the offending state in the least degree of calamity and misfortune, the offending individuals being chastised within lawful limits.[1]

The focus here is on the more significant obligation to preserve the peace and fight only when necessary. On the other hand, Vitoria recognized that war may break out and he constructed his summary in terms of the obligations governing a warring country, especially with respect to the limits regarding what it can do after one country has won.

Suárez also presented a summary of his just war theory:

> In order that war may be justly waged, certain conditions are to be observed and these may be brought under three heads. First, it must be waged by a legitimate power. Second, its cause must be just and right. Third, just methods should be used, that is, equity in the beginning of the war and the prosecution of it and in victory. . . . The reason of the general conclusion is that although war, in itself, is not an evil, yet on account of the many ills which it brings in its train, it is to be numbered among those undertakings which are often wrongly done. And thus it needs many circumstances to make it honest.[2]

The major way in which this summary differs from the previous one is that it focuses on the means of conducting war. That is, it focuses primarily on the *jus in bello*. Of special importance is Suárez's notation that even though war is not evil, the way it is conducted may cause it to become evil. One therefore needs to attend, in particular, to the circumstances in which it is conducted to make it just.

The conduct of the Christians during the Crusades frequently gave the lie to the moral teaching on the limits of war and violence. Zeal for the faith and hatred of the Muslims combined to blind most Christians so that they did not restrain their own conduct, much less evaluate it honestly. During and after the Protestant Reformation of the sixteenth century, there were many hideous wars of religion in which Christians fought each other to establish the purity of their doctrine. This was followed, primarily in Spain, by the Inquisition, which caused much suffering to many innocent people but was again justified by the need for purity of religion. Although during this time period the popes served as mediators in various wars, especially between France and England as well as many other nations, it remains the sad fact that the Church both participated in and encouraged much of the violence. Although the role of the Church during the Middle Ages was not all negative with respect to its participation in war and other forms of institutionalized violence, the Church nonetheless participated more and more in the affairs of state and at times became identified exclusively with particular rulers as they attempted to achieve their political ends, through both statecraft and war.

## THE MODERN CHURCH

Many popes in the modern age continued the role of mediator, especially during the many wars that occurred in Europe. Pius IX attempted to mediate the Franco-German War of 1870, but neither side seemed to wish to settle the dispute. In the aftermath of the war, the Catholic Church lost its territory in Italy known as the Papal States. While possession of this territory caused many problems, especially in the relations between the Catholic Church and Italy, nonetheless the loss of territorial sovereignty allowed future popes to be perceived as neutrals since they no longer had extensive territorial holdings or political entanglements to occupy their attention and set their political agenda.

Leo XIII, who served as pope from 1878 to 1903, was sought as a mediator in various disputes by Germany, Spain, England, Portugal, and Belgium. In his 1881 encyclical letter, *Diuturnum Illud*, Leo XIII suggested that the pope could serve as a mediator for international disputes. In 1889, he condemned the use of aggressive wars to settle national differences. He encouraged several peace conferences and, in 1900, performed a symbolic example of disarmament by melting down old swords and selling them as scrap iron.

Pius X became pope in 1903 as an arms race was beginning in Europe and hostility between nations was developing. In 1905, Pius X condemned strident nationalism and a policy of "might makes right." In spite of his efforts, though, Pius X was not able to persuade the nations of Europe to refrain from fighting, and in 1914 World War I broke out.

Benedict XV, whose papacy lasted from 1914 to 1922, continued the efforts of Pius X by appealing for peace among the nations. In his 1914 encyclical he proposed an armistice; in his Christmas message he attempted to arrange a truce, and in August 1917 he sent a note to various belligerents outlining definite proposals for peace. However, whether because of a perception of improper political interference on the part of the pope or because of religious prejudice, Benedict XV was not allowed to participate in helping to bring World War I to an end.

After Benedict's death in 1922, Pius XI assumed the papacy, which he held until his death in 1939. He continued his efforts and made many significant contributions to the development and preservation of peace. Pius XI spoke out against the delusion of preserving peace through armaments; critiqued nationalism, both economic and political; and urged that peace education programs be developed by the hierarchy. His focus on the need for internationalism and recognition of the unity of all people is summarized in the following quotation from his encyclical letter *Ubi Arcano Dei*:

> Love of country becomes merely an occasion, an added incentive to grave injustice, when true love of country is debased to the condition of an extreme nationalism, when we forget that all men are our brothers and members of the same great human family, and that other nations have an equal right with us both to life and to prosperity.[3]

Pope Pius XII succeeded Pius XI in 1939 and encountered many international crises and diplomatic challenges during his pontificate.

These included, but were not limited to, World War II, the Holocaust, and the development of nuclear weapons. Since Pius XII was one of the more prolific popes, we cannot offer an exhaustive survey of all of his statements on war and peace but will present several significant statements of his to obtain an overview of his orientation. Pope Pius XII continually placed before his various audiences the ideal of peace and the conditions necessary for peace as well as teaching the legitimate means to preserve peace. Wars, the pope felt, were caused by a type of spiritual anemia as well as a nonobservance of the laws of God and nature. Peace would come through a deepening of spirituality and a development of appropriate moral dispositions. Pius XII continually rooted his version of peace in observing the demands of justice and charity.

Pius XII made two important statements with respect to the kind of wars that could legitimately be fought. First, he continued the tradition of prohibiting wars of aggression. In his 1944 Christmas message, he indicated that the immorality of wars of aggression had become more evident than ever before. And in his 1948 Christmas message, he said:

> Every war of aggression against these goods which the Divine plan for peace obliges men unconditionally to respect and guarantee and accordingly to protect and defend is a sin, a crime, an outrage against the majesty of God, the Creator and Ordainer of the world.[4]

Second, he continued to teach the legitimacy of a war of self-defense and underscored the right, and even necessity, of a country to defend itself. This dimension of his teaching was reiterated several times during his pontificate.

For example, in his 1940 Christmas message, in discussing the premises for a new world order, Pius observed: "This conception [that might can create right] does not exclude the desire for the honorable improvement of conditions or the right to defend oneself if peaceable life has been attacked, or to repair the damage sustained thereby."[5] In his 1948 Christmas message, Pius XII said:

> A person threatened with an unjust aggression, or already its victim, may not remain passively indifferent, if one would think and act as befits Christians. All the more does the solidarity of the family of nations forbid others to behave as mere spectators, in an attitude of apathetic neutrality. Who will ever measure the harm already caused in the past by such indifference to war of aggression, which was quite alien to the Christian instinct?[6]

Later on in that same message, he stated:

> One thing, however, is certain: the commandment of peace is a matter of Divine Law. Its purpose is the protection of goods of humanity, inasmuch as they are gifts of the Creator. Among these goods are those of such importance

for society that it is perfectly lawful to defend them against unjust aggression. Their defense is even an obligation for the nations, as a whole, who have a duty not to abandon a nation that is attacked.[7]

The necessity of the ethical correctness of a war of defense was further recognized in an address on international medical law on 19 October 1953, in which Pius XII said: "Every war should be punished on the international plane unless it be demanded by the absolute necessity of self-defense against a very grave injustice affecting the whole community which cannot be prevented by other means."[8]

The right to self-defense also included the right to use atomic weapons. In a statement whose fractured syntax reflects the state of the pontiff's tortured soul, Pius observed in his 1956 Christmas message:

> The actual situation, which has no equivalent in the past, ought nevertheless to be clear to everyone. There is no further room for doubt about the purposes and message that lie behind tanks when they clash resoundingly across frontiers to distribute death and to force civilized peoples to a form of life that they distinctly abhor. When all the possible stages of negotiations and mediation are bypassed, and when the threat is made to use atomic arms to obtain concrete demands, whether these are justified or not, it becomes clear that, in present circumstances, there may come into existence in a nation a situation in which all hope of avoiding war becomes vain. In this situation, war of efficacious self-defense against unjust attacks, which is undertaken with hope of success, cannot be considered illicit.[9]

Another significant dimension of Pius XII's teachings is his statement on conscientious objection. In his 1956 Christmas message, he also said:

> If, therefore, a body representative of the people and the government—both having been chosen by free elections in the moment of extreme danger, decides, by legitimate instruments of internal and external policy, on defensive precautions, and carries out the plans which they consider necessary, it does not act immorally. Therefore, a Catholic citizen cannot invoke his own conscience in order to refuse to serve and fulfill those duties the law imposes. On this matter we feel that we are in perfect harmony with our predecessors, Leo XIII and Benedict XV, who never denied that obligation, but lamented the headlong armaments race and the moral dangers accompanying barracks life and urged, as we do likewise, general disarmament as an effective remedy.[10]

This statement contains two dimensions: first, as stated previously, a state has the right to declare war—even nuclear war—to defend itself; second, once the government has appropriately declared war, individuals may not invoke their conscience to exempt themselves from service to the country in fighting the war. The importance of this teaching is to remove the responsibility for such decision making from the individual and to place it on the shoulders of the state. Once the state has decided, the individual must conform to the authority of the state. Given the clarity of this statement and Pius's own valuing of ecclesiastical authority, it is no wonder that many people at the time felt it was impossible for a Catholic to be a conscientious objector to war in general or, more specifically, when a country had legitimately declared a war of self-defense.

However, the context in which war was conducted and the continued development of new and more powerful atomic weapons created a situation that gave rise to other considerations and to the beginnings of a reevaluation of the traditional teaching on war as well as the application of that teaching to the current situation.

## CONTEMPORARY PAPAL TEACHING

### John XXIII (reigned as pope 1958–1963)

The encyclical *Pacem in Terris*, written in 1963, was the first major statement on peace to be issued by a pope in many years. Pope John XXIII dealt with the problem of war and the promise of peace in the third section of this encyclical, which addressed the relations between states. He made two general points. First, truth and justice are the main norms by which the relations between states are to be regulated, and they are to produce an atmosphere of active solidarity so that states can work together to promote the national and international common good—"the sum total of those conditions of social living whereby men are enabled to achieve their own integral perfection more fully and more easily" (Paragraph 58). Second, Pope John argued that the arms race destroys truth and justice and, therefore, breaks down attempts to actualize solidarity among nations.

Pope John claimed that the arms race violates justice because it channels intellectual and economic resources into the development of weapons of destruction and consequently inhibits economic and social progress. Pope John also argued that the ever-increasing number of weapons has the likelihood of setting off a war, either accidentally or intentionally. He also suggested that the testing of nuclear weapons, an inherent part of the arms race, has the potential to jeopardize various kinds of life on the earth. In summary, the arms race deprives individuals and nations of the resources they need to develop their own common good and jeopardizes the well-being of people by increasing the likelihood of war and by harming the environment in which people live.

The more critical comment of Pope John, however, was directed toward nuclear war itself: "Therefore, in an age such as ours which prides itself on its atomic energy, it is contrary to reason to hold that war is now a suitable way to restore rights which have been violated."[11] Even though this translation has frequently been questioned and, despite the suggestion that it should be very narrowly interpreted, Pope John seriously challenged the moral viability of nuclear war. And that challenge was picked up by many individuals and sparked a reevaluation of war in Roman Catholic theology. Perhaps that is Pope John's greatest legacy to us: he encouraged the rethinking of the traditional ethic of war, and he was a prophet who stirred us out of a lethargy that accepted nuclear war as a means of vindicating rights.

## Paul VI (reigned as pope 1963–1978)

Pope Paul VI, in his 1967 encyclical *Populorum Progressio*, also spoke of the problem of war and violence. The primary focus of this encyclical was the social conditions necessary for achieving appropriate levels of development. Part of the problem addressed was the reality of social injustice and the search for the means to overcome it. In general, Pope Paul VI hoped to achieve development through structural reform and by promoting those social conditions that enhance human dignity. He also recognized, however, that injustice and dependency can make resorting to violence to achieve one's goals a serious temptation, and in regard to this he stated:

> We know, however, that a revolutionary uprising—save where there is manifest, long-standing tyranny which would do great damage to fundamental personal rights and dangerous harm to the common good of the country—produces new injustices, throws more elements out of balance and brings on new disasters. A real evil should not be fought against at the cost of greater misery.[12]

Although not directly addressed to the problem of war, these words do argue that recourse to violence typically does not resolve problems and, in fact, often creates more problems than it solves. However, Pope Paul provided no criteria for evaluating what many came to call a justified revolution or a justification for a war of national liberation. Although not necessarily applicable to the relationships between different sovereign nations, nonetheless the exception that Pope Paul presented stands in the tradition of the justified use of violence within the Roman Catholic moral tradition.

Pope Paul VI continued his critique of war through his statements on the arms race, disarmament, and development. Following very much in the line of Pope John XXIII, he linked peace with a reallocation of national resources to the poor and on behalf of the common good. For him, justice, which was the key to development, was the very means to peace.

In his 1976 World Day of Peace address, Pope Paul VI also critiqued the arms race in the following terms:

> What a loss in terms of education, culture, agriculture, health and civic life. True peace and life struggle on under an enormous and incalculable burden so that a peace based on the perpetual threat to life may be maintained and life may be defended by a constant threat to peace![13]

In a 1978 message to the United Nations, Pope Paul said:

> Resource to arms is a scandalous thing. The thought of disarmament on the
> other hand awakens great hope. The scandal is due to the crying dispropor-
> tion between the resources of money and mind that are put at the service of
> the dead and those that are devoted to the service of life. The hope is that, as
> military expenditures lessen, a substantial part of the immense resources
> they preempt today may be used for a vast project of development on a
> world scale.[14]

Paul VI's hope was that by eliminating the causes of injustice and by
promoting an authentic human development among all nations and peoples of the world, various forms of international cooperation would decrease the enmity that exists between different nations, and consequently,
peace would be achieved. We must always keep in mind Paul VI's im-
passioned plea at the United Nations: "No more war, war never again!
Never one against the other."

## John Paul II (reigned as pope 1978 to the present)

Pope John Paul II, himself the victim of terrorist violence (a 1981 assassi-
nation attempt), has proven to be an outspoken advocate for peace. On a
very practical level, he helped facilitate a dialogue that fostered a nonviolent solution to Poland's social crisis of the 1980s, resulting in a peaceful transition to a new political and economic system throughout Eastern
Europe. He has also offered to serve as a mediator in various disputes and
problematic areas existing between different nations. And while he has
demanded that priests and members of religious congregations do not directly intervene in political events, especially by holding public office,
nonetheless he himself has provided an interesting example of how one
might engage in political activity by leading the singing of nationalistic
songs while visiting Poland.

John Paul II has made two especially important statements on peace.
The first comes from his 1979 encyclical letter *Redemptor Hominis*:

> These words become charged with even stronger warning when we think
> that, instead of bread and cultural aid, the new states and nations awakening
> to independent life are being offered, sometimes in abundance, modern
> weapons and means of destruction placed at the service of armed conflicts
> and wars that are not so much a requirement for defending their just rights
> and their sovereignty but rather a form of chauvinism, imperialism and neo-
> colonialism of one kind or another. We all know well that the areas of misery
> and hunger on our globe could have been made fertile in a short time if the
> gigantic investments for armaments at the service of war and destruction
> had been changed into investments for food at the service of life.

For this reason the Church does not cease to implore each side of the two and to beg everybody in the name of God and in the name of man: do not kill! Do not prepare destruction and extermination for man! Think of your brothers and sisters who are suffering hunger and misery! Respect each one's dignity and freedom![15]

This quotation reflects a traditional emphasis in Catholic documents for the last forty years: increased military budgets have not only taken away money that could have been used for the development of farmlands or the procuring of food, thus ensuring that people will not be able to eat, but have also provided newer weapons with means of destruction rather than means of survival. The pope suggested that priority should be placed on the goals of relieving human hunger and suffering rather than preparing for the destruction of the human race.

When Pope John Paul II addressed the United Nations in October 1979, he said:

The ancients said: "Si vis pacem, para bellum." But can our age really believe that the breathtaking spiral of armaments is at the service of world peace? In alleging the threat of a potential enemy, is it really not rather the intention to keep for oneself a means of threat, in order to get the upper hand with the aid of one's own arsenal of destruction? Here too it is the dimension of peace that tends to vanish in favor of ever a new possible form of imperialism.[16]

The point that the pope made here is that the arms race, rather than being a form of national security, is actually a threat to the peace of the world and is simply a means of being able to continually threaten one's enemies. Also, in an important way, the pope linked the arms race and imperialism, for those who have the power of ultimate destruction may also be able to obtain the power to control the world. Such elements, the pope suggested, make peace impossible and cause it to vanish. Perhaps one can paraphrase the ancient wisdom by suggesting, especially in light of the previous quotation from his encyclical, that if we wish peace, we should prepare the earth so that we can harvest its riches and relieve hunger and suffering.

## CONTEMPORARY CHURCH DOCUMENTS

### Vatican Council II (1962–1965)

The convening of the Second Vatican Council provided the first occasion in almost a century for the Church as a whole to reflect on its situation in the modern world. Pope John XXIII wanted the Church to bring itself up to date, to address contemporary problems, and to take part in the discussion of the major questions of the day. For better or worse, one of the questions the Council had to address was the question of war.

Probably the most widely quoted statement from Vatican II with respect to war is that one should approach the evaluation of war "with an entirely new attitude."[17] The Council's primary reason for such a new attitude was the development of weapons that "can inflict massive and indiscriminate destruction far exceeding the bounds of legitimate defense."[18] It is within this framework that the Council Fathers made the following pronouncement that, together with the condemnation of abortion, is the only condemnation to be found in the entire body of the Council documents.

> With these truths in mind, this most holy synod makes its own the condemnations of total wars already pronounced by recent popes, and issues the following declaration: Any act of war aimed indiscriminately at the destruction of entire cities or extensive areas, along with their population, is a crime against God and man himself. It merits unequivocal and unhesitating condemnation.[19]

However, the Council Fathers did not, with this strong condemnation, revoke the right of national self-defense. They said:

> Certainly, war has not been rooted out of human affairs. As long as the danger of war remains and there is no competent and sufficiently powerful authority at the international level, governments cannot be denied the right to legitimate defense once every means of peaceful settlement has been exhausted. Therefore, government authorities and others who share public responsibilities have an obligation to protect the welfare of the people entrusted to their care and to conduct such grave matters soberly.[20]

Together with this validation of the legitimacy of self-defense, the Council also made a positive statement about members of the military: "Those who are pledged to the service as members of its armed forces should regard themselves as agents of security and freedom on behalf of their people. As long as they fulfill this role properly, they are making a genuine contribution to the establishment of peace."[21]

Even though the Council made these positive statements about the legitimacy of war as a means of self-defense when all other means have failed and gave a positive sanction to the role of individuals who are in the military, it nonetheless upheld the necessity to evaluate morally the waging of war.

> It is one thing to undertake military action for the just defense of the people, and something else again to seek the subjugation of other nations. Nor does the possession of war potential make every military or political use of it law-

ful. Neither does the mere fact that war has unhappily begun mean that all is fair between the warring parties.[22]

And remembering many of the atrocities that occurred, specifically in World War II in Nazi Germany, but anticipating new atrocities—especially the increased use of torture by the military—the Council said the following:

> Contemplating this melancholy state of humanity, the Council wishes to recall first of all the permanent binding force of universal natural law and its all-embracing principles. Man's conscience itself gives an ever more emphatic voice to these principles. Therefore, actions which deliberately conflict with these same principles, as well as others commanding such actions, are criminal. Blind obedience cannot excuse those who yield to them. Among such must first be counted those actions designed for the methodological extermination of an entire people, nation, or ethnic minority. These actions must be vehemently condemned as horrendous crimes. The courage of those who openly and fearlessly resist such commands merits supreme commendation.[23]

But the most surprising aspect of the Council's deliberation is reflected in its teachings on pacifism and conscientious objection. In part, they represent a stark departure from the teaching of Pius XII, but on the other hand they reflect the development of a new form of thought with regard to war and peace initiated by John XXIII and continued by Paul VI. The Council stated:

> For this reason, all Christians are urgently summoned "to practice the truth in love" (Eph. 4:15) and to join with all true peacemakers in pleading for peace and bringing it about. Motivated by this same spirit, we cannot fail to praise those who renounce the use of violence in the vindication of their right and who resort to methods of defense which are otherwise available to weaker parties too, provided that this can be done without injury to the rights and duties of others or of the community itself.[24]

The Council then added:

> Moreover, it seems right that laws make human provisions for the case of those who for reasons of conscience refuse to bear arms, provided, however, that they accept some other form of service to the human community.[25]

This represents a dramatic step forward. For the first time an official Church teaching of an ecumenical Council recognized the right of conscientious objection, and praise is given to those who would use the strategy of nonviolence or perhaps adopt a pacifist lifestyle. The Council recognized that there is a plurality of opinions with respect to war and peace within the Catholic community, and it sanctioned a variety of ways of responding to this critical issue. On the one hand, the Council reaffirmed, in light of the lack of an international authority, the right of self-defense, but on the other hand it positively praised those who seek ways other than war to resolve international conflict. The Council also stated its deep concern about modern means of warfare and the extreme destruction it can bring about, and it also expressed serious moral reservations about the arms race as a means of ensuring lasting peace. Furthermore, following many other official teachings, it recognized that the arms race siphons money from other worthy social concerns and from the poor and, in fact, creates a trap from which humankind may not escape.

While the Council provided no final resolution with respect to the question of war or peace, perhaps more importantly it recognized that one needs to rethink the issue of war and peace with a new added truth in light of the changed circumstances of modern warfare, and it also gave clear praise and sanction to the rights of those who choose to be conscientious objectors or pacifists.

### Report of the Holy See to the United Nations General Assembly

This very interesting document, presented in 1977 by Monsignor Giovanni Cheli, then permanent observer for the Holy See at the United Nations, focused on disarmament but also presented some extremely strong views about the means of conducting war. The document argued that the arms race is unjust because it amounts to a violation of rights by giving primacy to force, and then the stockpiling of weapons becomes an excuse for recourse to the increased exercise of naked power. The arms race is also unjust because it is an act of theft that takes money that could be used to fund projects to advance the common good and instead uses that money for the manufacture and stockpiling of arms. The document argued that such a use of funds for arms while many vital needs remain unsatisfied, especially in developing countries, is basically an act of criminal aggression. Further, the document asserted that the arms race is an absurdity because it is a means disproportionate to the end and, therefore, cannot guarantee security. Since there is already an overabundance of weapons, the arms race does not increase security, and additional weapons present only the means for overkill. The document stated: "The arms race institutionalizes disorder and thus becomes a *perversion of peace.*"[26]

The report clearly condemns the arms race, first in the name of peace, which the arms race does not secure, and second in the name of both natural morality and the gospel ideal. The document applied two principles in coming to this judgment. First, there is no longer a proportion between the harm caused by the arms race and the values to be protected, and therefore, it is better to suffer injustice than to defend oneself, or at least to defend oneself by means such as these. Second, when the principal use of weapons is not defense but aggression, the rationale for their use loses its reason for being, its justification, and its legitimacy. The document then concluded:

> In this kind of activity, we no longer have simply a cold war but an offensive action, *an unacceptable act of aggression and oppression.*[27]

## THE AMERICAN CHURCH

The American Catholic church was founded as a church of immigrants who often found their allegiance to this country challenged. This challenge, heightened by the Nativist and Know-Nothing movements of the nineteenth century, as well as continuing anti-Catholic prejudices that reached a climax in the 1928 presidential campaign of Al Smith, encouraged a stance of almost hyper-patriotism among American Catholics that frequently led to an uncritical acceptance of American foreign and domestic policies. As Catholic assimilation into the American mainstream continued, symbolized most clearly by the election of John F. Kennedy as the first Catholic president, Catholics began to feel more secure in their position here, and this led to a more relaxed relationship with the culture and the policies of the government. The Vietnam War, a protracted conflict that engaged U.S. troops in futile combat that claimed 50,000 American lives, was the watershed for a break with uncritical patriotism. Many of the most outspoken antiwar activists were Catholics and some were members of the clergy. Such a shift in perspective is also reflected in various pastoral letters and statements of individual bishops as will be seen in reviewing the following statements.

### Pastoral Letters

#### Human Life in Our Day

This 1968 letter of the American bishops continued the tradition of Pius XII by condemning without qualification wars of aggression. The letter stated:

> Whatever case there may have seemed to exist in other times for wars fought for the domination of another nation, such a case can no longer be imagined given the circumstances of modern warfare, the heightened sense of mutuality and the increasingly available humane means to the realization of that mutuality.[28]

The bishops also endorsed the Second Vatican Council's condemnation of wars fought without limitation. In the concluding section, the American bishops developed a positive teaching on conscientious objection. In validating the search of one's own conscience, especially with respect to the morality of participation in war, they said:

> As witnesses to a spiritual tradition which accepts enlightened conscience, even when honestly mistaken, as the immediate arbiter of moral decisions, we can only feel reassured by this evidence of individual responsibility and the decline of uncritical conformism to patterns, some of which included strong moral elements, to be sure, but also included political, social, cultural and like controls not necessarily in conformity with the mind and heart of the Church. If war is ever to be outlawed, and replaced by a more humane and enlightened institution to regulate conflicts among nations, institutions rooted in the notion of universal common good, it will be because the citizens of this and other nations have rejected the tendency of exaggerated nationalism and insisted on principles of non-violent political and civil action in both the domestic and international spheres.[29]

The American bishops went on to endorse the statements of Vatican II that praised those who renounced the use of violence to vindicate their rights and suggested, also in light of Vatican II, that provision be made for those who refuse to bear arms. But then, in a surprising move, they went further than the Council and followed the logic of the just war theory to its logical conclusion:

> The present laws of this country, however, provide only for those whose reasons of conscience are grounded in a total rejection of use of military force. This form of conscience objection deserves the legal protection made for it but we consider that the time has come to urge that similar considerations be given to those whose consciences are more personal and specific.
>
> We therefore recommend a modification of the Selective Service Act making it possible, although not easy, for so-called selective conscientious objectors to refuse—without fear of imprisonment or loss of citizenship—to serve in wars which they consider unjust or in branches of service (e.g., the strategic nuclear forces) which would subject them to actions contrary to deeply held moral convictions about indiscriminate killing. Some other form of service to the human community should be required of those so exempted.[30]

The option of selective objection is a logical conclusion of the just war theory, but many were surprised when the American bishops explicitly announced their acceptance of such a position and also suggested that it be made legal. That is, of course, in direct contradiction to the teaching already mentioned of Pius XII that when a country has legitimately declared a war, no one can object to it. This teaching of the American bishops represented a dramatic development in the teachings about war.

This letter also focused on one specific weapon: the neutron bomb. The bishops observed:

Nothing more dramatic would suggest the anti-life direction of technological warfare than the neutron bomb; one philosopher declares that the manner in which you will leave entire cities intact, but totally without life, makes it, perhaps, the symbol of our civilization. It would be perverse indeed if the Christian conscience were to be unconcerned or mute in the face of the multiple moral aspects of these wearisome prospects.[31]

Unfortunately, this dramatic statement was largely forgotten when discussions of the development and use of this weapon took place in the late 1970s and early 1980s. This particular weapon does have the advantage, however, of revealing our true priorities: property is more important than life.

The fact that the United States has shifted to a volunteer army and currently has no draft in place may seem to question the relevance of this teaching on selective objection. However, since eighteen-year-olds are required to register and since a draft could be reestablished, such a teaching retains its moral relevance. Additionally, the teaching on selective obedience is most relevant for those volunteering to serve in the armed forces or those on active duty. The teaching encourages individuals to examine carefully the war effort to determine for themselves if it conforms to the just war doctrine. Such an emphasis on individual moral responsibility is particularly important in times such as those following the events of 11 September 2001. While the urge for revenge and vengeance is understandable, more so is the need for moral examination of the response to these events. It is too easy to be swept up in patriotic fervor and the heat of anger—justified as that anger might be—and to let moral evaluation fall by the wayside. Hence the importance of the doctrine of selective obedience, which insists on the responsibility of individuals to morally evaluate the situation and come to their own conclusions.

## To Live As Christ Jesus

This 1976 pastoral letter focused, in part, on the use of nuclear weapons. The important element in this teaching of the American bishops is the following statement:

> With respect to nuclear weapons, at least those with massive destructive capability, the first imperative is to prevent their use. As possessors of a vast nuclear arsenal, we must also be aware that not only is it wrong to attack civilian populations, but it is also wrong to threaten to attack them as part of a strategy of deterrence. We urge the continued development and implementation of policies which seek to bring these weapons more securely under control, progressively reduce their presence in the world, and ultimately remove them entirely.[32]

This statement strikes directly at the heart of the deterrence theory by arguing that it is wrong to threaten to attack civilian populations or, in the terms of the just war theory, to attack innocents or noncombatants. It would have been even more interesting if the American bishops had drawn out specific behavioral consequences for Catholics, especially those who are involved in some way in either the production or the potential use of such weapons.

## The United States Conference of Catholic Bishops

The United States Conference of Catholic Bishops (USCCB), formed in 2000 by a uniting of the United States Catholic Conference (USCC) and the National Conference of Catholic Bishops (NCCB), is the administrative arm of the U.S. Catholic Bishops and is responsible for developing statements that reflect current Catholic teachings. Statements discussed here were presented by the two separate conferences before their merger in 2000 and will be discussed under their previous names.

A variety of statements have been made by the USCCB, either as an organization or by individuals speaking on its behalf, that are related to issues of war and peace. While some of these simply repeat material that we have previously mentioned, other statements carry this teaching a bit further.

For example, an October 1969 statement called "Catholic Conscientious Objection" basically repeated the teaching found in the pastoral letter *On Human Life in Our Day*. But in addition to this wider promulgation of the teaching, the USCC also made two recommendations: (1) that each diocese initiate or cooperate in providing draft information and counseling and (2) that Catholic organizations that could qualify as alternative service agencies consider applying for that status and support and provide meaningful employment for the conscientious objector. The importance of these recommendations is that they initiated on a diocesan level a means of implementing this particular position on conscientious objection. This position also indicated the appropriateness of the role of individual conscience in determining whether one is or is not a conscientious objector and provided official support for those individuals who choose the route of conscientious objection.

A 1978 USCC statement titled "The Gospel of Peace and the Danger of War" indicated that the primary moral imperative at the time was that "the arms race must be stopped and the reduction of armaments must be achieved." Several objectives were then identified: the superpower arms race must be brought under control both quantitatively and qualitatively, the proliferation of nuclear weapons must be restrained, and restrictions must be placed on the rapid growth of conventional arms sales in the world. The document concluded with the following exhortation:

> To pursue peace in the political process requires courage; at times it means taking risks for peace. The Church in a competent and careful manner must encourage reasonable risks for peace. To risk requires a degree of faith, and faith, in turn, is based on the hope that comes from prayer. As the Church in this nation, we seek to be a moral voice placing restraints on war, a prophetic voice calling for peace, and a prayerful community which has the courage to work for peace.[33]

On occasion, individuals spoke on behalf of the United States Catholic Conference, and two instances of this were extremely important for the ethical debate on war and peace in the United States Catholic community. The first presentation was testimony on the SALT II Treaty (an arms limitation treaty between the United States and the Soviet Union) to the Senate Foreign Relations Committee in 1976 by the late Cardinal Krol of Philadelphia. In this testimony, Cardinal Krol made several important statements with respect to Roman Catholic teachings on war and peace. While Cardinal Krol was speaking on behalf of the USCC, his brother bishops, and the Catholics of the nation, it is too much to expect that everyone would agree with everything he said. What is important to keep in mind, however, is that Cardinal Krol was one of the more conservative cardinals of the country and was generally perceived to be very much on the side of the status quo, both politically and socially. His Senate testimony included these observations:

> This role requires me to speak the truth plainly. The Catholic bishops of this country believe that too long have we Americans been preoccupied with preparations for war. Too long have we been guided by the false criterion of equivalence or superiority of armaments; too long have we allowed other nations to virtually dictate how much we should spend on stockpiling weapons of destruction. Is it not time that we concentrate our efforts on peace rather than war? Is it not time that we take that first step toward peace; gradual, bilateral, negotiated disarmament?[34]

In this statement Cardinal Krol challenged some of our widely accepted national priorities, especially those supported by the defense industry. He suggested that for a long time we have been looking in the wrong direction and have been guided by false criteria for security.

Another important statement in his testimony follows:

> In a nuclear age, the moral sanctions against war have taken on a qualitatively new character. From Pius XII to John Paul II, the moral argument is clear: the nuclear arms race is to be unreservedly condemned and the political process of arms control and disarmament is to be supported by the Christian community.[35]

This is an extremely strong statement because it says that the nuclear arms race is to be condemned. One could assume that certain behavioral implications would flow from such a condemnation. For example, does this condemnation mean that individuals may no longer participate in building nuclear weapons? Does it mean that individuals may not serve in a branch of the armed services that would bomb another country with this weapon? Does it mean that military chaplains should teach Catholic soldiers under their jurisdiction that they may no longer participate in a form of military service related to nuclear weapons and that they should disobey the commands of their superiors? These are very challenging questions, but they seem to be logical consequences of Cardinal Krol's statement.

Cardinal Krol made one other lengthy statement that deserves quotation because of the seriousness of the implications that flow from it:

> The moral paradox of deterrence is that its purpose is to prevent the use of nuclear weapons, but it does so by an expressed threat to attack the civilian population of one's adversary. Such a threat runs directly counter to the central moral affirmation of the Christian teaching on war: that innocent lives are not open to direct attack. The complexity of that moral dilemma is reflected in the statement on deterrence of the American bishops in 1976: With respect to nuclear weapons, at least those with massive destructive capability, the first imperative is to prevent their use. As possessors of a vast nuclear arsenal, we must also be aware that not only is it wrong to attack civilian population but it is also wrong to threaten to attack them as part of a strategy of deterrence. We urge the continued development and implementation of policies which seek to bring these weapons more securely under control, progressively reduce their presence in the world, and ultimately remove them entirely (To Live As Christ Jesus, 1976).
>
> The moral judgment of this statement is that not only the *use* of nuclear weapons is wrong but so is the *declared* intent to use them in our deterrence policy. This explains the Catholic dissatisfaction with nuclear deterrence and the urgency of the Catholic demand that the nuclear arms race be reversed. It is of the utmost importance that negotiations proceed to meaningful and continued reductions in nuclear stockpiles, and eventually to the phasing out altogether of nuclear deterrence and the threat of mutually assured destruction.
>
> As long as there is hope of this occurring, Catholic moral teaching is willing, while negotiations proceed, to tolerate the possession of nuclear weapons for deterrence as the lesser of two evils. If that hope were to disappear, the moral attitude of the Catholic Church would almost certainly have to shift to one of uncompromising condemnation of both use and possession of such weapons.[36]

This quotation contains a very succinct and accurate summary of Roman Catholic teaching on deterrence policy. The critical comment, however, is in the last paragraph, and the basic issue is determining whether at the present time the modest hope that Cardinal Krol held out is in fact true or not. One can certainly make an argument that breaking off the SALT II talks, the dramatic increase in our military budget, and the aggressive, hard line being taken toward many nations indicates that this hope may be disappearing. One also needs to be concerned about the increased discussions regarding the possibility of winning a nuclear war. Such statements were made during the unsuccessful 1980 presidential campaign of the elder George Bush, and they were continued during the Reagan administration. However, Cardinal Krol presented an interesting test that must be applied to our situation—and moral conclusions must be drawn from that.

While the end of the Cold War and the voluntary and agreed upon destruction of large numbers of nuclear weapons have in fact reduced much of the tension and terror under which so many lived for so long a time, the reality of nuclear weapons and other weapons of mass destruction remains. While deterrence may not be quite the issue it was at the time of Krol's testimony, we still experience nuclear proliferation by many nations as well as the possibility of nuclear weapons being used as instruments of terrorism.

Another individual who gave testimony on behalf of the United States Catholic Conference is Reverend J. Bryan Hehir, then the associate secretary for International Justice and Peace and currently the president of Catholic Charities USA. Again, while not everyone would agree with Father Hehir's testimony to the House Committee on Armed Services presented in March 1980, nonetheless it is important as a statement that reflects at least some degree of consensus with the USCC and, therefore, indicates at least the feeling, if not the formal position, of the USCC. In this testimony, Father Hehir made one important statement that articulated his perception of the state of the debate over war and peace in current Catholic theology. While we will return to Father Hehir's contributions later in this book, it is important to put this quotation forward as his summary, on behalf of the USCC, of the state of the debate.

> While it would be too much to conclude that Catholicism has adopted an in-principle position of pacifism as its sole response to modern war, it is possible to see that the nuclear age, and its attendant awesome danger, has moved Catholic moral teaching to affirm only a quite narrow justification of resort to arms. The shift of perspective in turn shapes the following principles which are at the heart of contemporary Catholic teaching on modern warfare:
>
> 1. Condemnation of the arms race as "an utterly treacherous trap for humanity" and "a danger and injustice, a theft from the poor and a folly." Correlatively, the Church has continually supported efforts of disarmament which would proceed "at an equal pace according to agreement and backed up by authentic and workable safeguards."
>
> 2. Condemnation of total war and the use of weapons which "can inflict immense and indiscriminate havoc that goes far beyond bounds of legitimate defense."

3. Support for the positions of conscientious objection and selective conscientious objection as means by which individuals can fulfill their duty to scrutinize whether specific forms of warfare are legitimate and justifiable.

4. Recognition of the right of the state "to legitimate defense once every means of peaceful settlement has been exhausted." The meaning of legitimate defense, however, is shaped by the previous three principles.[37]

What is important about this statement, in addition to the concise articulation of the current Catholic teaching, is its recognition and affirmation that there has been a shift in the teaching on war in Catholic theology. These new positions have been sanctioned at the highest official levels of Catholicism and has received support from many moral theologians as well as many other interested Catholic lay people. The basis for this shift undoubtedly has been the status of contemporary warfare, especially with respect to nuclear weapons. Another dimension of this shift of approach has come from the impact of the arms race on civilian populations and the devoting of more and more time, energy, and money to the creation of weapons that, although designated as defensive, possess the potential to destroy the entire world. And again, while not drawing any specific conclusion with reference to a particular situation, Father Hehir's testimony provided a framework for the analysis of many situations nonetheless.

## SUMMARY

Several important conclusions follow from this survey of Roman Catholic teaching on war and peace.

1. There is a right of nations to defend themselves through force if all other means have failed to resolve the dispute. This right to defend oneself exists primarily because there is no international agency with sufficient power to serve both as a mediator of disputes and as a guarantor of the enforcement of treaties.

2. However, there has been a major shift in how war is perceived. It is the teaching of the Catholic Church at the present time that only a defensive war can be justified. That is, the right to defend oneself, mentioned in the first point, may be exercised only when one is defending rights that have been violated. Total war and wars that seek to punish a neighboring country, for example, or wars that seek to expand one's boundaries are prohibited. Only a defensive war can be justified according to current Catholic teaching. One must consider carefully the so-called Bush Doctrine of the legitimacy of preemptive strikes in light of this teaching.

3. Contrary to the teaching of Pius XII, the Catholic Church now recognizes, at the highest levels, the right of an individual Catholic citizen to be either a complete conscientious objector or, more interestingly, to be a selective conscientious objector. The Catholic position on selective conscientious objection is a logical conclusion from the traditional use of just war categories to evaluate the morality of war. What is interesting about the acceptance of this possibility within the Roman Catholic tradition is that such a position is politically dangerous and at present contrary to U.S. law. The American Catholic Church, in particular, has gone on record as recommending that legal recourse be established for those who wish to assume this particular posture during a particular war.

4. Another important conclusion of current Catholic teaching on war has to do with the condemnation of the arms race. The arms race is seen as a waste of money because it puts one's hopes for security in a false and unsafe place; it is also seen as a form of theft in that money that could be spent for more important social goods is diverted toward destruction. This teaching stretches back to the views of Pius XII and has continued through the teachings of John Paul II.

5. Current Roman Catholic teaching also recognizes that there are grave moral difficulties with the development of nuclear weapons and the conducting of war using nuclear weapons. One of the difficulties has to do with the strategy of deterrence, which threatens to destroy civilian populations, as well as the possible use of nuclear weapons that would destroy a disproportionate number of innocent people but that also have the potential to destroy the entire world. Nuclear weapons have been the major factor in initiating a reevaluation of the Roman Catholic Church's teaching on war. They present unique problems in that they threaten the destruction of the entire world, but they also have caused individuals to live in constant terror, and the cost of their production has been responsible for diverting money from important social projects. The possibility of the use of these weapons in terrorist attacks reveals yet another shift in the continued impact of nuclear weapons on our lives. While even traditional just war theory would condemn such use of these weapons, we seem to be unable to make this case persuasively. The nuclear legacy continues to haunt us.

The Roman Catholic community must determine what, if any, behavioral implications for the members of the Church will flow from these teachings. The drawing of specific conclusions from these general principles will be extremely problematic and will cause a great deal of dissension. Nonetheless, it can reasonably be argued that the task of the Church as a moral teacher is to draw conclusions that offer specific guidance to its members. This moral direction must extend to individuals who work in defense-related industries as well as to members of the armed services, including the chaplains. Also the Catholic Church must begin to think through what it means for the ordinary citizen to support, at least indirectly, nuclear warfare through paying taxes. One bishop, for example, recommended that Catholics withhold a portion of their income tax as a protest against the spending of that money on weapons of destruction. Such a recommendation is extremely problematic, not only because it is illegal, but also because it suggests that individuals have a significant responsibility in determining the political direction of their nation and that such a determination can be exercised in a very significant way: through the withholding of financial support for government projects.

The 1970s and 1980s would prove to be extremely difficult decades for Roman Catholics with respect to the problem of war and peace. It was imperative at that time that the Catholic Church provide appropriate guidance for conducting the debate on war and peace. Its leadership was called upon to engage in the search for practical direction for how its members should conduct themselves in these critical and dangerous times. And this was precisely the task that the Catholic community undertook in 1983 in producing the pastoral letter *The Challenge of Peace*.

# 3

+

# American Theological
# Reflection on War and Peace

Many American Catholic theologians have examined the morality of war. Such was the case especially in the 1950s when the pressure of the Cold War made it appear likely that an actual war was a possibility. This discussion was also stimulated by the continued developments in nuclear weaponry, especially the transition from an atomic to a hydrogen bomb and the new modes of delivery. Most of the theological analysis in the 1950s and early 1960s was in the context of papal teachings and the Cold War. As the Church began to change and develop, especially after Vatican Council II, there was also a shift in the moral analysis of the problem of war. This transition came about dramatically with the encyclical letter *Pacem in Terris* of John XXIII. This pope's initiatives on peace and his analysis of nuclear war spurred a whole new development in the moral analysis of war. One significant dimension was the shift from focusing only on the morality of war to developing a perspective focusing on peace and promoting peace. While this perspective was certainly not lacking in the earlier teaching, the traditional orientation saw peace as the conclusion of the just war teaching. The new orientation suggested that peace was the point of departure and the context in which the morality of war might be analyzed.

This section of the book will summarize several of the teachings of major Catholic theologians with respect to the morality of war. This survey will provide an orientation to both the content of the analysis as well as how that analysis has changed over the past years.

## JOHN C. FORD, S.J. (1902–1989)

John Ford's analysis of the morality of war and of practices within the conducting of war began with an acceptance of the possibility of war's being moral and its being conducted in a moral fashion. In a significant 1944 article titled "The Morality of Obliteration Bombing," this American Jesuit stated his position as follows:

> I do not intend to discuss here the question: Can any modern war be morally justified? The overwhelming majority of Catholic theologians would answer, I am sure, that there can be a justifiable modern war. And the practically unanimous voice of American Catholicism, including that of the hierarchy, assures us that we are fighting a just war at present. I accept that position.[1]

In his analysis of the morality of war and its practices, Ford distinguished between what a confessor ought to do practically and what general moral principles ought to be and imply with respect to the moral evaluation of war. In determining confessional practice, Ford emphasized the conscience of the individual, especially given the fact that there may not be a clear Church teaching or clear moral consensus on a particular act or situation. For example, in 1941 Ford said that if the infallible Church has not spoken and will not speak on the justice of a given war, and when Catholic hierarchies of opposing enemy nations speak on it and give opposite answers, and when moral theologians are still forming their opinions, "the very least we can say is that, as far as confessional practice is concerned, the sincere conscientious objector is entitled to the freedom of his conscience. The fact that he is Catholic does not make it wrong for him to be a conscientious objector, too."[2]

Ford continued this reasoning by saying:

> The impression made upon the present writer by reading the foregoing literature (and much more like it) is that the application of our moral principles to the modern world leaves so much to be desired that we are not in a position to impose obligations on the consciences of the individual, whether he be a soldier with a bayonet or a conscientious objector, *except in the cases where violation of natural law is clear.*[3]

And again in an article before the strategy and tactics of World War II were fully in place, Ford suggested that it seemed utterly inhuman to allow the bombing of civilians from the air. But then he went on to say, "That problem remains to be answered; and, as we said last year, in the meantime pilots and bombardiers may continue to obey the orders of their superior officers, except in cases where it is *certain* that an unjustifiable act on the innocent is being made."[4]

The problem of bombing (obliteration bombing, in particular) led Ford in 1944 to focus on that particular problem in a lengthy article in *Theological Studies*. While this article focused explicitly on the problem of the morality of obliteration bombing, it was also important in terms of his argument about the morality of the conduct of war and how one constructs a moral argument.

Again, Ford proposed a twofold analysis: confessional practice and moral evaluation. With respect to the confessional, Ford again argued that it is quite appropriate for a confessor to give absolution to a bombardier who felt forced to carry out orders to take part in obliteration bombing unless, of course, the penitent is convinced of the immorality of the practice. The reasons for this include that the problem is a comparatively new one; there may not be specific norms laid down by ecclesiastical authorities; there is a well-established rule based on the presumption that favors the following of commands by the civil authorities; and, as stated earlier, Ford thought that application of moral principles to war leaves so much to be desired that we should not impose obligations on the conscience of individuals unless there is a certain violation of natural law. Having thus dealt with the practical problem of how to handle individuals who confess participation in such bombing, Ford next developed his analysis that convinced him of the immorality of the practice of obliteration bombing.

Ford defined obliteration bombing in the following way:

> Obliteration bombing is the strategic bombing, by means of incendiaries and explosives, of industrial centers of population in which the target to be wiped out is not a definite factory, bridge, or similar object, but a large area of a whole city, comprising one-third to two-thirds of its whole built-up area, and including by design the residential districts of working men and their families.[5]

Ford used two traditional principles of the just war theory to argue against this practice: the immunity of noncombatants in warfare and the violation of the principle of double effect.

Ford recognized that, given the context of modern war, it can be difficult to distinguish combatants from noncombatants. Nonetheless, he argued that such a distinction is valid and, therefore, the traditional principle of the innocence of noncombatants and the impermissibility of killing them still held. He basically argued that even though it may be difficult to draw the line, that difficulty did not obliterate the line between innocence and guilt. Even though there might be some uncertainty in the application of principles, that in itself was not an argument that the principles are, in fact, inapplicable. Finally, in a very incisive comment, Ford identified the root problem: "Is it not evident that the most radical and significant change of all in modern warfare is not the increased cooperation of civilians behind the lines of the armed forces, but the enormously increased power of the armed forces to reach behind the lines and attack civilians indiscriminately, whether they are thus cooperating or not?"[6] Thus, the real problem, in Ford's opinion, was not the obliteration of the distinction between combatants or noncombatants or even a difficulty in drawing the distinction, but rather the increased capacity to bomb cities. Ford also developed an empirical argument, based on population studies, that a large number of categories of working people cannot be reconstituted to switch their category from noncombatants to combatants. Ford recognized that many working people will, in fact, be indirectly or in some other fashion aiding the war cause. To expect anything else is simply unrealistic. Yet, Ford was quite content to argue that some indirect cooperation does not constitute a moral sanction justifying a change in the status of a person from noncombatant to combatant.

Ford also used the principle of double effect to condemn obliteration bombing. He counterargued that the principle should not be applied in this particular situation. First, he looked at the question of intent and asked: "Is it possible to employ this procedure without directly intending the damage to innocent civilians and their property?"[7]

Focusing primarily on civilians, Ford answered this question by saying:

> Looking at obliteration bombing as it actually takes place, can we say that the maiming and death of hundreds of thousands of innocent persons, which is its immediate result, is not directly intended, but merely permitted? Is it possible psychologically and honestly for the leaders who have developed and ordered the employment of this strategy to say that they do not intend any harm to innocent civilians?[8]

This answer led Ford to conclude that it is impossible to engage in obliteration bombing without directly intending the destruction of, and harm to, innocent civilians. This orientation was strengthened by his quoting of various British and American documents that argued that the purpose of obliteration bombing was to undermine the morale of the Germans and to bring terror and devastation to the enemy nation. Ford argued that it is impossible to make civilian terrorization or the undermining of civilian morale an object of bombing without having a direct intent to injure and kill civilians. "If one intends the end, terror, one cannot escape intending the principal means of obtaining that end, namely, the injury and death of civilians."[9]

Ford's other argument against the use of the double effect principle focused on proportionality, and his basic point was that obliteration bombing violates proportionality because the alleged proportionate causes that justify the bombing are "speculative, future, and problematical, while the evil effect is definite, widespread, certain, and immediate."[10] This summarized Ford's perception that the justification of obliteration bombing—it will help win the war, it will shorten the war, it will save soldiers' lives, it will enable the Allies to liberate Europe and feed the starving people sooner was simply a rationalization of military strategy that served as a pretext for destroying civilian populations to win the war. Again, what Ford appropriately focused on here was not individual acts of bombing, but the strategy of obliteration and terrorism as such. And it was this accepted strategy that Ford saw as leading to disproportionate effects that cannot be justified by the variety of ends one might cite as supposedly overriding these moral objections.

Ford concluded his analysis by saying:

> Obliteration bombing, as defined, is an immoral attack on the rights of the innocent. It includes a direct intent to do them injury. Even if this were not true, it would still be immoral, because no proportionate cause could justify the evil done; and to make it legitimate would soon lead the world to the immoral barbarity of total war. The voice of the Pope and the fundamental laws of the charity of Christ confirm this condemnation.[11]

The significant dimension of Ford's orientation is that, while he accepted that a war can be just, and that the principles of the just war and other moral principles for analyzing its legitimacy can be valid, nevertheless, he was quite willing to apply these principles to specific tactics used in the war and to draw ethical conclusions. The other critical dimension of Ford's analysis was his careful distinction between the conscience of an individual who is participating in the war and the moral evaluation of the policy as a whole. Relying in part on a methodology that looked to ecclesiastical authority for ultimate validation of an argument, he nonetheless was quite willing to formulate an argument that could lead the ecclesiastical authorities to make a moral judgment on a certain policy that would then be binding on all individuals. While Ford recognized that certain practices can get utterly out of hand and lead to the total immorality of a particular war or the immorality of the way in which the war is conducted, he accepted the idea that war can be a moral enterprise and focused his moral analysis on the practices of war.

## GERALD KELLY, S.J. (1904–1964)

Gerald Kelly continued the tradition of analyzing the problems of modern war, especially modern war conducted with atomic weapons, within a framework of the just war theory and the principle of double effect. In his comments on the problem of war, this American Jesuit inaugurated the process of thinking through the morality of atomic warfare. What was also significant about Kelly's analysis, though not surprising in light of the context of the Cold War in which he developed it, is the role of war with respect to its preserving the rights of Christian civilization. While part of his analysis was directed to a commentary on other opinions proposed by moral theologians, he stated quite clearly several presuppositions that led him to his conclusion on the legitimacy of the use of atomic weapons.

> All of us would undoubtedly agree that atomic weapons should be outlawed. Yet, in the supposition of the conflict between theistic, peace-seeking nations and atheistic, aggressive forces, such a compact is hardly possible. The atheist would choose his own weapon. Granted this supposition, I agree with Father Connell when he says that the use of the hydrogen bomb by the defensive nations can be justified. I also agree that when such a weapon is directed toward a military target, the damage to civilians can be explained as indirect, even though it be terribly devastating. Finally, I think that Father McCarthy is wrong in saying that there can be no proportionate reason for permitting this devastation; for, in a supposition I am making (which is certainly not unrealistic), there is a question of preserving the lives, as well as the religious and civic liberty, of more than half the world. I think that this is a sufficient compensating reason for almost any amount of damage indirectly inflicted on the citizens of the atheistic/communistic lesser nations.
>
> In expressing this opinion, I am not condoning unnecessary damage. We can fervently (or perhaps vainly) hope that a future war will not involve the unnecessary damage that characterized the last war. But, granted that the objectives are military targets, and granted the necessity of eliminating them in order to resist atheistic aggression, I am of the opinion that the concomitant civilian devastation can be justified. I would apply this opinion either to the use of a single H-bomb on the target of supreme importance or to the use of A-bombs on a number of less important military targets.[12]

Important in this moral analysis is the ideological context in which it occurred. For example, we might consider objecting by raising the question: would the same argument take place if the aggressor nation were a Christian nation? It is unclear what the relevant criterion is. Is it the fact that the country is atheistic that justifies bombing it, or is it the fact that it is both atheistic and aggressive, or is it the fact that it is merely aggressive?

Kelly did not abandon the distinction between combatants and noncombatants, nor did he accept the concept of total war. What he did, though, was to countenance a wider range of destruction of persons and property than did Ford. He based his judgments about permissibility on the difficulty of distinguishing precisely between nonmilitary and military targets and between combatants and noncombatants. Even though the targets should be military, the use of atomic weapons in a war for the survival of our civilization, he argued, can be justified even though this means an enormous destruction of civilian lives.

Kelly also made a brief, but interesting, comment on what has come to be called the morality of a first strike with nuclear weapons, an argument that could today be seen as supporting the current doctrine of preemptive strike:

> I also agree with Father Walsh that, once the United States was certain of an imminent attack by an aggressor with an atomic bomb, our government would have no obligation to await the attack before using atomic bombs on the military targets of the aggressor nation. In fact, I should think that there would be an obligation not to await such an attack.[13]

Again, the critical feature of Kelly's argumentation was the continued acceptance of the categories of just war theory with respect to nuclear warfare and the continued extension of traditional moral principles into the analysis of modern warfare. The interesting difference between Kelly's analysis and Ford's analysis is the intrusion of the explicit ideological context in which the argument is cast. Ford, for example, was quite willing to argue that the U.S. policy of obliteration bombing was quite immoral. Kelly, on the other hand, saw the role of the United States as the preserver of Christian civilization and argued, therefore, that almost any amount of destruction would justify the survival of the free world. What we can learn from this is the necessity of being alert to how a moral argument can be shaped or controlled, wittingly or unwittingly, by an ideological perspective.

## JOHN COURTNEY MURRAY, S.J. (1904–1967)

Among the many significant contributions that John Courtney Murray made to theology, and the American theological enterprise in particular, was his continued reliance on and development of the natural law as a means for enhancing and resolving significant issues of our time. Murray was convinced that reason could work its way through the tangles of social difficulties and international conflicts and lead people to valid ideas on which all could agree and to which all could assent. Murray's discussion of war provided us with three important contributions: a summary statement of the just war theory in the late 1950s, a summary statement of the functions of a just war theory, and a statement on the role of conscience in applying the categories of the just war theories, especially in relation to selective conscientious objection.

In his summary of the just war theory, Murray followed quite closely the thought of Pius XII, but he also displayed his acuity as a moral theologian by clarifying and interpreting that thought. The first general principle Murray affirmed was that all wars of aggression, whether just or unjust, are morally proscribed. This principle stated that even redressing the violation of a nation's legal rights is not in itself a justification for war. Murray argued, in support of the pope's orientation, that the use of force cannot now be a moral means for the redress of violated legal rights. No state may now take the cause of justice into its own hands: "Whatever the grievance of the state may be, and however objectionable it may find the status quo, warfare undertaken on the solemn decision of the national state is an immoral means for settling the grievance and for altering existing conditions."[14]

There were two basic reasons for this principle. First, the increased violence of war in the present condition disqualified it as an apt and proportionate means for resolving international conflicts and even resolving unjust grievances. Second, the continued observance of a right to wage war as an attribute of national sovereignty would block the development of an international community with juridical power.

The second general principle was that a defensive war to oppose and defeat injustice is morally admissible both in principle and in fact. Under this principle, Murray stated four qualifications. First, the war must be imposed on a nation by an obvious and extremely grave injustice. Second, it must be, in fact, the last resort of the nation. Third, there must be a twofold proportionality: (1) "Consideration must be given to the proportion between the damage suffered in consequence of the perpetration of a grave injustice, and the damages that would be let loose by a war to repress the injustice" and (2) "Pius XII requires another estimate of another proportion, between the evils unleashed by war and what he calls 'the solid probability of success' in the forceful repression of unjust action."[15] Fourth, a limitation must be placed on the use of force. In part, this principle related to the kinds of weapons used, especially if they would utterly destroy all human life within their radius of action, but it also maintained the distinction between combatant and noncombatant.

A third general principle of Murray's formulation of the just war theory was the legitimacy of defense preparations, which he justified with two reasons. First, as a matter of fact, no international authority possesses a monopoly on the use of armed force when there is an international dispute. Second, Murray acknowledged the persistence of violence and lack of principle in the resolution of disputes. Because of these situations the right to self-defense cannot be denied to any state.

The fourth principle is Pius XII's rejection of the validity of conscientious objection. Pius argued that when the government acts in a matter

that is not immoral, the citizen may not make appeal to his own conscience as grounds for refusing to render his service.

Having developed this framework, Murray then went on to analyze issues in the application of the theory. Murray argued that the doctrine basically boils down to, especially with reference to the terms of public debate, a justification of limited war. The principle of limitation stated that
legitimate defense against injustice must also take into account that force
is a last resort to be used only to repel an injury. For Murray, the critical
issue was the setting of a public policy that will enable war to be conducted in a limited fashion. The question of how to limit the extent of violence emerged as the core of the moral problem of modern warfare. Murray spelled out this orientation forcefully and clearly in describing how it
can be used with respect to evaluating the moral issues in the conducting
of nuclear war.

> In other words, since limited nuclear war may be a necessity, it must be made
> a possibility. Its possibility must be created. And the creation of its possibil-
> ity requires the work of intelligence, and the development of manifold ac-
> tion, on a whole series of policy levels—political (foreign and domestic),
> diplomatic, military, technological, scientific, fiscal, etc., with the important
> inclusion of levels of public opinion and public education. To say that the
> possibility of limited war cannot be created by intelligence and energy, under
> the direction of a moral imperative, is to succumb to some sort of determin-
> ism in human affairs.[16]

To do this Murray suggested that one must construct a kind of model
of limited war in which the relationships between different levels of policy making are clearly established. For example, one must determine the
relationship between foreign policy, military policy, and fiscal policy,
among others, and then determine which of these takes priority and what
their inner relationship is. The other element in the development of a
moral policy on war is to attempt to think through where an armed conflict may occur and how that conflict might be limited in those situations
with respect to political intentions and military necessities. Thus, for Murray, the moral problem of conducting a just war was to determine exactly
how power was to be applied, directed, and limited. This requires the setting of appropriate policy so that correct determinations can be made.

A third element that Murray examined was the role of individual conscience in evaluating the decision of a state to conduct war. Murray basically held that the just war theory provided a means of moral analysis of
the use of force in the legitimate self-defense of a state. To do this one
must also take into consideration certain political and military dimensions of the situation, but such consideration in itself did not make a judgment about the morality of the war purely political. As Murray said, "It is

a judgment reached within a moral universe, and the final reason for it is of the moral order."[17] The tension then, for Murray, was between what he identified as the conscience of the laws and the conscience of the individual. He argued that when the decision-making process of a community has been exercised and a decision reached, a preliminary measure of internal authority must be conceded to that decision by the citizens. This orientation assumed that the state is both a moral and a political agent and that when it exercises its decision-making power, its decision is binding on the citizens and they should unite behind that decision to implement it. With respect to the evaluation of war, then, the citizen must first concede a degree of justice to the common political decision. If citizens should dissent, the burden of proof for that dissent is upon their shoulders, for they must overcome the decision of the state. The moral tension here is between the appropriateness of the state with respect to decision-making power and the recognition that citizens must not surrender their conscience to the state. Stated another way, Murray argued that no political society should grant absolute rights to the individual conscience. He saw this as a type of rank individualism and a misunderstanding of the nature of the political community. On the other hand, the political community must appropriately respect the conscience of the individual. This, of course, presupposed that the consciences of the citizens are both formed and informed.

For Murray, the just war theory was first of all a means to mediate between two extremes that he viewed as operative in American society: absolute pacifism in peacetime and extremes of violence in war. The just war theory provided a means to exercise some discrimination in the use of force. Second, the just war theory assumed that military decisions are functions of political decisions and that political decisions must be seen as moral decisions. Third, because of political decisions or moral decisions, there was a necessity for both the state and the citizen to engage in both public and private reflection upon the morality of a particular use of force in a particular situation. As stated earlier, the primary issue was the limitation of force, not the necessary rejection of it. Thus, for Murray, the critical issue was the informed political–moral debate that must engage both the citizen and the state before a war begins so that one can best determine how that war is to be conducted in a moral fashion. This was premised upon the state's having the right to self-defense but also recognized that, from a moral point of view, the state may not do whatever it wishes to defend itself.

Murray made one other point that is of particular relevance to the policy of deterrence: "With us, if deterrence fails, and this massive exchange occurs, that is the end. We have no policy after that, except stubbornly to maintain that it is up to the enemy, and not us, to surrender unconditionally."[18] In this short sentence, Murray pointed out an egregious failing of the policy of deterrence: What do we do if it doesn't work? Perhaps for Murray the moral issue here was not the use of a policy of deterrence but the narrowness with which such policy was conceived and its exclusive reliance upon unacceptable levels of force as the linchpin of the strategy. Perhaps he found this perspective problematic because of its narrow and uncritical use of force. But whatever his justification for that statement, Murray said something here that is of continuing relevance and that needs to be dealt with seriously as we continue to examine the morality of conducting a war, particularly as a response to terrorist attacks.

## PAUL HANLEY FURFEY (1896–1992)

The late Monsignor Paul Hanley Furfey, a priest and sociologist at the Catholic University of America, was the author of numerous books and had been involved in various aspects of Catholic activism. His involvement ranged from his own personal involvement with the Catholic Worker movement and the establishment of various houses of hospitality and settlement houses, to his own social and moral analysis of Catholicism and the culture in which it exists in his many writings over several decades. During the course of his career, he made many significant contributions to the evaluation of moral issues relating to war, the draft, pacifism, and nationalism.

One of his consistent themes was a critique of exaggerated nationalism that he defined as placing loyalty to the country above loyalty to God.[19] Exaggerated nationalism is a distortion of patriotism that leads people to engage in war. More importantly, though, Furfey argued that exaggerated nationalism can deaden one's conscience so that what is apparently wrong becomes seen as what is obviously right. Furfey argued that each individual must evaluate the morality of a particular war but that if one is possessed with the spirit of exaggerated nationalism, this evaluation becomes almost impossible because the individual gives his or her loyalty to the wrong reality—the state.

Furfey did not hesitate in using this insight to evaluate the behavior of American Catholic bishops during World War II. He criticized them quite severely for not protesting the saturation bombing of German cities during World War II, as well as for approving the dropping of the atomic bomb on Hiroshima and Nagasaki. He also applied this insight to evaluating the war in Vietnam and basically suggested that loyalty to the country inhibited American Catholics from morally evaluating what was going on. Furfey summarized this orientation in a very appealing way in his commentary on a statement made by Cardinal Spellman during the Vietnam War:

> Sometimes the morality of a war is not merely overlooked but is positively distorted. . . . Cardinal Spellman once settled the moral problem of the Vietnam War to his own satisfaction by paraphrasing Decatur: "Right or wrong, it's my country." This was clearly an explicit repudiation of Christian morality as the supreme norm of conduct. Yet one may be sure that the cardinal was unaware of this repudiation. Doubtless he simply repressed the thought that Decatur's principle was the negation of Christian moral doctrine. Thus he was able to agree with the super patriots without being conscious of any disloyalty to Catholic teaching. This attitude is doubtless quite common. In wartime, without doubt, many Catholics follow the principle that whatever the government commands is the citizen's duty, and they follow this principle without being consciously disloyal to the moral teaching of their Church.[20]

Furfey gave two reasons why Catholics surrender their conscience to the state. First, they tend to accept a popular code of morality that focuses on private sins to be avoided rather than virtues to be practiced. And because this code defines the sins to be avoided in terms of individual morality, the tradition has never clearly articulated a social code of morality or shown how various virtues could lead to social action. Second, moral theology did not develop a strong sense of social sins or social virtues and, therefore, individuals turned to the state by virtue of its laws or its governmental decisions to obtain their code of social morality. Since Christians were now taking their moral lead from the state, it should come as no surprise that the state's requirements were not submitted to moral analysis. Political actions and judgments were not seen as appropriate objects of moral analysis.

> Furfey continued this analysis in his evaluation of war: The usual failure to apply Christian principles to public issues is particularly evident in time of war. Few persons are willing to face the elementary truth that war is a moral problem, that a war may be either just or unjust, and that it is the Christian's duty to refuse to support a war when he is morally certain that it is unjust.[21]

In saying this, Furfey was not defining himself as a pacifist. In fact, in an early book he argued: "It is certain beyond any doubt that a Catholic cannot be a conscientious objector in the sense of the absolute pacifists."[22] In other words, no Catholic may assert a priori that all wars are wrong and announce his intention of abstaining from any war at all regardless of the issues involved. He also argued elsewhere that nonviolence is not to be a substitute for the ordinary agencies of law enforcement and that nonviolence is not a universal principle, but a characteristically Christian policy.[23]

According to Furfey, Christianity does not mean the repudiation of physical force under all circumstances: "In the New Testament there is no suggestion that they [Christians] should put down their arms and allow anarchy to prevail."[24] However, Furfey does suggest that nonviolence, defined as the absence of retaliation when it is to be expected, is a characteristic Christian technique for modifying the social order. Importantly here, he defines it as a strategy as opposed to a philosophy of life.

Although not a pacifist, Furfey was very insistent that Catholics take seriously the obligation to evaluate war morally. He used the tradition of the just war theory for his analysis, but what is different about his approach is that he took many of the issues seriously and applied them not only to the conduct of the enemy but also to the conduct of his own nation. This approach led him to see World War II and the Vietnam War as unjust wars because of the way in which they were conducted. He logically argued that if individuals morally evaluate the decision of the government to fight a war or examine the conduct of their government while fighting a war and find moral problems, then they are obliged to be conscientious objectors to that particular war. Interestingly enough, Furfey did not limit his notion of an obligation to object to the war only to those who are subject to the draft, for he also put this obligation upon others whom he called civilian conscientious objectors. Thus he pursued with logical and moral relentlessness the obligation of a Christian to oppose immoral governmental policies, especially during the conduct of war, regardless of an individual's social position.

While Furfey was not a pacifist, did not accept the opinion that all war is wrong, and continued to use the just war categories as a means of analysis, he also put a high priority, from a Christian point of view, on a strategy of nonviolence and demanded a rigorous application of Christian moral principles to the actions and policies of government. Such an orientation led him, from a practical point of view, to argue that almost no war conducted in a present context could be viewed as just.

## DOROTHY DAY AND THE CATHOLIC WORKER

The Catholic Worker movement continues to be an important source of the articulation of concern for the needs of the poor as well as for a continuing critique of society and government policies. Founded by the twentieth-century social activists Peter Maurin and Dorothy Day, the Catholic Worker provided houses of hospitality where the poor could find food and shelter and furnished an example of how Christianity could be practiced when taken with utmost seriousness. The Catholic Worker houses in both urban and agricultural areas were to be viewed as exemplary communities that would provide a vision of Christianity for the rest of the Catholic community. This unique social movement came about from the continuing collaboration between Maurin and Day. Day was a fellow traveler with socialists and other radicals during the early 1900s. She learned much from extended sessions of traveling and living with the poor and experiencing the hardships they had to endure, as well as a career in journalism and writing. She was dissatisfied to some extent with her life, though, and did not find direction in it until after the birth of her daughter, at which time she began to see that many of her hopes and aspirations would be fulfilled in Catholicism. But here, too, her hopes did not reach fruition until she met Peter Maurin, a French peasant and wandering teacher. Maurin had been developing his own vision of Christianity and, together with Dorothy Day, was able to articulate this vision and give it a concrete form in the newspaper *The Catholic Worker*, in the various houses of hospitality, and in the social activism they undertook.

Sociologist Patricia McNeal suggested that three basic touchstones formed the heart of the Catholic Worker vision. First, a type of eschatological radicalism suggested that the vision and goals of the Catholic Worker movement, with respect to the harmony and union of all people, could only be achieved at the end of time when Christ would return. The followers of the movement were to live in expectation of this event and were to live it out in their lifestyle. Second, the movement developed a sense of Christian personalism that focused on putting love into practice in the arena of history, as well as emphasized a Christian's ability to turn from being captured by the reality of the world to embracing the reality of the spirit. Third, there was a consistent critique of both nationalism and capitalism that was based on a sense of dissatisfaction with a nation built around competition and the glorification of struggle. Although it is unclear whether Maurin himself was a pacifist, Dorothy Day argued that pacifism flowed clearly from the principles they articulated and was the fulfillment of their vision.[25]

Another important dimension of the Catholic Worker orientation toward pacifism was its reading of the events in the late 1930s and early 1940s. The members felt, as did many other individuals, that the developing sources of war were simply a replay of the causes of World War I and that the war would be used to protect the investments of bankers and to develop profits for capitalists and industrialists. Further, it would be encouraged by communists and other visionaries who saw war as a means of overthrowing current political structures to set up ones that would advance their ideology.[26]

The general anarchistic philosophy of the Catholic Worker movement, drawing on both Christian and political sources, also led to several practical consequences based on its pacifist stance. Its general orientation was to try to have as few interactions with the institutions of the state as possible. This had significant consequences with respect to not paying taxes, and it also advanced the idea that individuals should not even register for the draft, as well as find other ways of avoiding cooperation with the entire structure set up to enlist people in the war machine.

More importantly, the pacifism and nonviolence of Dorothy Day and the Catholic Worker movement were based on its Christian vision and sense of personalism that took seriously the command to love one's enemies. The Catholic Worker movement tried to live out as faithfully as possible this unique moral principle in Christianity by not cooperating with violence and by not harming other people. Dorothy Day saw no way other than that of pacifism and nonviolence. Although the Catholic Workers originally set out their position in the context of the just war theory and although it was, technically, more a form of selective conscientious objection, the Catholic Worker movement nonetheless began to base its position regarding pacifism more and more clearly upon the gospel injunction of loving one's neighbor and not harming one's enemy. This stand, articulated in its paper, caused the movement a considerable degree of pain as well as a loss of membership, particularly during World War II. Not all of the members of the loosely associated houses of hospitality subscribed to the idea of pacifism to the same extent as Dorothy Day did. Consequently, many people left the Worker movement because of the peculiarities of Dorothy Day's theology and because of her acceptance of total pacifism. Some reconciliation was achieved after World War II, but Dorothy Day maintained her insistence that those who subscribed to the movement must also subscribe to pacifism.

Dorothy Day's total embrace of radical Christianity and her living out of it in both a life and a strategy of nonviolence led her to take positions and support people that made her unpopular in many circles. Her stand was not without a significant cost and seemed many times to put her at the mercy of those who would take advantage of her. Nevertheless, Dorothy Day remained faithful to her principles of pacifism, and she sought to keep the Catholic Worker movement as a sign of how one could both be a pacifist and live in a contemporary society. The movement she established continues to serve, even after her death, as a sign of hope to people who wish to pursue peace and make nonviolence a viable strategy and philosophy of life.

## THOMAS MERTON (1915–1968)

Playing off Merton's own self-description, one author called him "a prophet in the belly of a paradox." Thomas Merton was at least a paradoxical figure: a monk, but an activist; a contemplative, yet an astute political commentator; removed from the world, but having tremendous social influence through his writings and letters; and finally, not a pacifist, but totally against modern war.

Merton's contribution to the moral analysis of war is very significant. This section will focus on why Merton did not consider himself a pacifist, his moral analysis of war, his reflections on nuclear war, and a summary of his own perspective on peacemaking and war-making.

Merton asserted quite clearly: "If a pacifist is one who believes that all war is always morally wrong and always has been wrong, then I am not a pacifist."[27] Such a position, however, did not prohibit him from becoming a noncombatant conscientious objector during World War II or from conducting a very strenuous moral analysis critiquing the continued reliance on war and violence as a means of achieving peace. A more nuanced version of his thought is the following statement:

> Characteristic of theological thought, both Protestant and Catholic, is the idea that the *presence of nuclear weapons does nothing to alter the traditional just war theory.* I am not a "pacifist" in the sense that I would reject even the *theory* of the just war. I agree that even today a just war might *theoretically* be possible. But I also think we must take into account a totally new situation in which the danger of any war escalating to all-out proportions makes it imperative to find other ways of resolving international conflicts. In practice the just war theory has become irrelevant.[28]

Thus Merton might fall under the label of those who are called nuclear pacifists—those individuals who argue that the presence of nuclear weapons has made it impossible for any war to be just because of the destructive power of nuclear weapons that would be used in that war.

The fact that Merton did not see pacifism as a moral obligation does not mean that he was indifferent to the moral obligation of all Christians to be peacemakers:

> It must however be stated quite clearly and without compromise that the duty of the Christian as a peacemaker is not to be confused with a kind of quietistic inertia that is indifferent to injustice, accepts any kind of disorder, compromises with error and with evil, and gives in to every pressure in order to maintain "peace at any price." The Christian knows well, or should know well, that peace is not possible on such terms. Peace demands the most heroic labor and the most difficult sacrifice. It demands greater heroism than war. It demands greater fidelity to the truth and a much more perfect purity of conscience.[29]

This orientation places a severe moral obligation on the conscience of each Christian to engage in pursuing peace and to reject the seduction and illusions of survival presented by those who think that our survival lies with war and the pursuit of the means that can be used in war. Merton also provided a fairly consistent and thorough critique of contemporary war, especially nuclear war.

Again we must keep in mind that on a theoretical level Merton did not rule out the possibility of the legitimate use of violent means to defend oneself or the possibility of a nation engaging in war. However, on a practical level, he fairly well ruled out the use of war. He clearly argued that total war was immoral. "It is the unanimous judgment of all really serious religious, philosophical, social psychological thought today that total war (whether nuclear or conventional) is both immoral and suicidal. This is so clear that it seems to require little discussion or proof."[30] Merton further argued that even the theologians who still argue that war itself can be a solution to international conflict agree that total war must be condemned not only as immoral but also as impractical and eventually self-defeating. He also restated the issue by claiming that it is not simply the case that atomic and nuclear weapons are immoral, but rather that any use of terrorism or total annihilation is unjust no matter what weapons are employed to carry out that policy.

Merton further specified why the just war categories are irrelevant:

The Popes have not merely been trying to say that nuclear war is not nice, but that it upsets traditional Catholic norms of morality of war. In plain language this is an essentially new kind of war and one in which the old concept of the "just war" is irrelevant because the necessary conditions for such a war no longer exist. A war of total annihilation simply cannot be considered a "just war," no matter how good the cause for which it is undertaken.[31]

Merton also spoke to the heart of the position of the Catholic Church on nuclear war:

It is commonly said, even by Catholics, that "the Church has never condemned a nuclear war," which is completely false. Of course the Pope has never pronounced an *ex cathedra* definition which would formally outlaw nuclear war. Why should he? Does every *infima species* of mortal sin need to be defined and denounced by the extraordinary magisterium? Do we now need an *ex cathedra* fulmination against adultery before Catholics will believe themselves bound in conscience to keep the sixth commandment? There is no need for nuclear war to be solemnly outlawed by an extraordinary definition. It should not even need to be condemned by the ordinary papal teaching. In fact, however, it has been so condemned.[32]

Merton used the occasion of an essay on the Nazi Gestapo officer Adolf Eichmann to make one of his more perceptive and sharp comments about war and the decision-making process involved in launching nuclear weapons:

It is the sane ones, the well-adapted ones, who can without qualms and without nausea aim the missiles and press the buttons that will initiate the great festival of destruction that they, *the sane ones*, have prepared. What makes us so sure, after all, that the danger comes from a psychotic getting into a position to fire the first shot in a nuclear war? Psychotics will be suspect. The sane ones will keep them far from the button. No one suspects the sane, and the sane ones will have *perfectly good reasons*, logical, well-adjusted reasons, for firing the shot. They will be obeying sane orders that have come sanely down the chain of command. And because of their sanity they will have no qualms at all. When the missiles take off, then, *it will be no mistake.*[33]

Merton quite appropriately attacked the concept of sanity that allowed continued discussions of nuclear war to occur, and in his sarcastic way he began to expose and undermine the mindset that allows such thinking both to occur and to be perceived as sane. The problem, he indicated, is that we are taking our concept of sanity from our society, and although that has been done in the past, it is becoming clear that Christians can no longer define sanity in a way that other members of society do.

This dedication to Christian sanity led Merton deeper and deeper into the reality behind Christianity and consequently sharpened his commitment to peace and to nonviolence as both a philosophy and a strategy. He had frequent concerns about the direction in which the peace movement was going in the United States, particularly during the Vietnam War and especially when individuals began burning themselves to death as a protest against that war. Still, he realized that the direction was the correct one, and he pursued his own efforts at promoting peacemaking and continued his writing, even though he was silenced for this for a time by his own superiors. His fidelity to the cause of peace and his eloquent wisdom remain with us as a magnificent legacy from the solitude of Thomas Merton.

## DANIEL BERRIGAN, S.J.

Among those individuals who captured the imagination of many in the peace movement during the Vietnam War were the brothers Berrigan. These two men, Philip, a Josephite who died in 2002, and Daniel, brothers, priests, and members of religious orders, succeeded in articulating a vision of peace and escalating the strategy of nonviolence, from the pouring of blood and napalm on draft records to living as a fugitive from federal authorities as a symbol of resistance to unjust authority. While both brothers were extremely active in the peace movement, this section will focus primarily on Daniel.

Daniel Berrigan has a long history of involvement in a variety of social activism, especially regarding work with and on behalf of poor people and minority groups. Also, early in his training he was exposed to the French Worker Priest Movement, which made a tremendous impact on his own thinking. In the early 1960s, he took part in freedom rides to achieve the integration of interstate buses. He also was involved to a large degree in the developing liturgical movement, which also significantly influenced his own thought insofar as he saw that the liturgy was a sacrament through which the mystery of humanity's redemption might be acted out and achieved. Finally, Berrigan was eventually exiled to Latin America so that he could be removed from his activities in New York. This experience served only to radicalize him further, as he was put in contact with many progressive groups in Latin America and saw new possibilities for resistance and new justifications for undertaking resistance to the government here.

Two other influences that were very significant for Berrigan—in addition to the ongoing presence of his brother Philip—were the Catholic Worker movement and the person of Thomas Merton. It is interesting that we find in Daniel Berrigan a coalescing of these two other strands of thought within Catholicism: the social apostolate and the critique of society from a monastic viewpoint. Berrigan had long been involved with the Catholic Worker movement and was influenced significantly by its vision of work with the poor, its pacifism, and its confrontation with the powers of state. And it was at a retreat conducted by Thomas Merton that Berrigan began to develop his own theology of resistance.

Berrigan's journey into civil disobedience and his rejection of many of the institutions of the United States, including the judicial and the executive branches, began out of a sense of frustration that he had exhausted all of the legitimate and traditional means for social reform that were at his disposal. He continued to speak, to write, and to engage in traditional acts of nonviolent protest, but to no avail. He also saw that the evil present in society, especially as this related to the poor, minorities, and the conduct of the war, was increasing. Finally, after continuing conversations with his brother Philip as well as his own reflection and prayer, he saw that he had to act and began by participating in the raid upon the office of the draft board raid at Catonsville, Maryland. His journey into civil disobedience continued when he realized that he could not in good conscience submit to the power that wished to send him to jail, because he saw that power as an unjust power, one intent on evil rather than good. He felt that he could not submit and thereupon assumed the role of a cleric in hiding. The FBI pursued him for several months before he was captured and sentenced to jail.

Daniel Berrigan has, as evidenced in his writings, undergone a most remarkable and dramatic transformation of thought and person. His early writings, the spirit of which is best captured in his first major book *The Bride*, almost portray the Church as outside the human world.[34] He is wrestling with the problem of the relationship between the Church and the world, and at this early period in his development he does not have an easy means of bringing together the sacred and the secular. This more transcendent view of the Church is modified in his later development by moving toward seeing the Church as an agent of change and as having a prophetic dimension. The images that he used at that time suggested that Christians must be a kind of living procession proceeding from the altar into the world. Consequently, he described the Eucharist as a kind of ferment of redemptive action within humanity.

The liturgy in this perspective is a living out of the law of love within one's place in the world as a means of transforming it. In reliving the mystery of Christ in the liturgy, individuals are to release again into the life around them the energy of God's love and forgiveness, which is the power that can redirect us and serve as an agent of our conversion and the transformation of the world. Finally, Berrigan saw that it will be necessary for the Church to take the radical stand of a prophet against society because what the Church sees in society is a radical denial of its message. This vision led Berrigan to recognize that our faith cannot be reduced to our culture, and that our civil citizenship must be different from our membership in the body of Christ. If the Church is to avoid disappearing into the contemporary equivalent of the Roman legions, it must be willing to make a clear declaration of where its values are and what the practical implications of these are for the life of its members. In his book *No Bars to Manhood* Berrigan said:

> No, God implies, there are times so evil that the first and indeed the only genuinely prophetic function is to cast down the images of injustice and death that claim man as victim. No, the times were judged by God; evil beyond cure. Only a new beginning would suffice.[35]

For Berrigan, then, two elements serve as the foundation for his activities: liturgical and biblical. The liturgical dimension presents as its goal to communicate the mystery of the death and resurrection of Jesus to the community so that it can be transformed into the new creation. In this sense, social action becomes the exterior expression of the key interior reality of liturgical experience: redemption. It is the acting out of the new creation by making it present within the context of one's everyday life. For Berrigan, social action is the concrete living out of the reality of the Eucharist, the transformation of the bread of one's everyday life into the bread of one's eternal life.

The biblical dimension of Berrigan's thought, particularly in his recent commentaries on biblical books and themes, provides the motivation and criteria for his actions. The Christian Scriptures in particular, as well as the writings of the prophets from the Jewish Scriptures, provide both a vision of the kind of actions one can perform as well as the virtues and reality that those actions ought to bring about. The Christian life is to be an acting out of the parables of Jesus, a living out of the Sermon on the Mount, the entire Christian Scripture, by declaring certain forms and styles of life to be null and void so that it will be possible to initiate a new creation, a new beginning. Action based on biblical inspiration can both point to the need for a new beginning as well as begin to initiate it by incarnating the vision and the reality that will make it possible.

Berrigan continues in much the same vein by living a life of service to his fellow humans. He worked with dying patients in a cancer hospital, he continues to write poetry and theological reflections upon the state of America, and he continues to engage in acts of resistance to the growing militarization of this country. In many ways he has become a thorn in the side of the power establishment of America because he refuses to stop speaking. He refuses to let people forget that they are in danger of being destroyed both by their own complacency as well as by their own compliance with the war machine that seeks to destroy. Berrigan serves as a continual witness to the evil that is present in our culture and society and continues to call all members of society to a lifestyle of nonviolence.

Berrigan's literary output continues; his social action continues; his commitment to the cause of peace and nonviolence continues. Berrigan, now in his eighties, is no longer the cult figure that once attracted hundreds of thousands of young people to follow the cause of peace. Yet he continues to be a leading spokesperson for the cause of peace in the United States, trying to focus our attention on what our lifestyle will bring us if we do not reorder our priorities. In many ways, all of Berrigan's work is but a commentary on the meditation he provided at Catonsville to interpret the significance of the burning of draft files with napalm:

> We shall beyond doubt be placed behind bars for some portion of our natural lives in consequence of our inability to live and die content in the plagued city, to say "peace, peace" when there is no peace, to keep the poor poor, the thirsty and hungry thirsty and hungry. Our apologies, good friends, for the fracture of good order, the burning of paper instead of children, the angering of the orderlies in the front parlor of the charnel house. We could not, so help us God, do otherwise. For we are sick at heart; our hearts give us no rest for thinking of the Land of Burning Children and for thinking of that other Child of whom the poet Luke speaks.
>
> We have chosen to say with the gift of our liberty, if necessary our lives: the violence stops here, the death stops here, the suppression of the truth stops here, this war stops here. Redeem the times.[36]

## J. BRYAN HEHIR

J. Bryan Hehir, a priest of the archdiocese of Boston, was the associate secretary for the Office of International Peace and Justice for the United

States Catholic Conference and is currently the president of Catholic Charities USA. In his many articles, Hehir continues to use the just war theory and specifically apply it to contemporary military and political problems, especially focusing on strategy. While many of his past public statements have been made on behalf of the USCCB, formerly the USCC, nonetheless they do represent his own personal thought. Hehir identified two moral problems that relate to the conduct of war: (1) Can the taking of human life for political purposes be justified? (2) How can moral doctrines and strategic doctrines be related?

Hehir is of the opinion that the just war theory can answer these questions positively, and in providing his analysis he also enters into a dialogue with another option: pacifism. The question of strategy is of particular importance to Hehir for three reasons: (1) in its strategic policy a nation states its intention of what it will or will not do, (2) strategic formulations are the means by which choices are shaped for the political leader, and (3) strategy provides the bases for determining which structural forces will be used to implement the decisions. Because of this, a primary moral problem on which Hehir focused is that of deterrence.

Hehir, however, is particularly concerned with affirming the validity and appropriateness of the just war theory. He does this first because of the continued Church tradition of the legitimate use of violent means to defend against violations of a state's rights:

> To assert the right of states to defend themselves without providing a moral framework for the assertions is to leave the road open to the indiscriminate use of force. The assertion requires an ethical calculus defining both the legitimate and the limited means which keep the use of force within the moral universe.[37]

Hehir relies upon the tradition of just war thought as developed in papal and conciliar teaching, but he also recognizes that it provides the moral logic needed to determine when and how this right of defense may be implemented. He also argues that the just war theory provides a measure of flexibility to respond to a variety of situations. He recognizes that the just war theory begins with premises that are held in common with pacifists: the sacredness of life, the realization that war is not exclusively a technical or political problem, a presumption against force, and the necessity of limiting the use of violence. What Hehir argues here is not only an affirmation of the legitimacy and even appropriateness of the use of force within the Catholic community, but also the necessity of recognizing that these premises can lead to a variety of conclusions, only one of which is something that resembles the just war theory. Hehir recognizes the moral pluralism present within the Catholic community and in fact illustrates this by the

American bishops' teaching on the legitimacy of both conscientious objection and selective conscientious objection to war. He argues that there can be both pacifists and just war theorists in the same ecclesial community but concludes that the same person cannot hold both of these theories simultaneously. He then further heightens the policy dimension of this pluralism by raising the question of what the public position of the Church should be. That in part is answered by his ecclesiology, which basically follows Murray's orientation that the Church has a role in setting the terms for the public debate of policy. Hehir does not forget that the Church must also speak exclusively to its own constituency and must occasionally utter a prophetic word. He is more concerned, however, with keeping the Church engaged in the process of public debate and policy analysis, and therefore, he continues to see the just war theory as an appropriate means by which the Church can engage in public policy discussions.

In testimony before the House Committee on Armed Services, with specific reference to the 1981 Defense Appropriation Act, Father Hehir, on behalf of the USCCB, argued that he was unconvinced that a limited nuclear war could be fought within the confines of a just war ethic. His specific conclusion from this premise was that moral priority must be placed on the nonuse of nuclear weapons and that counterforce capability, especially with respect to the development of the MX missile, should therefore not go forward. Because he was unconvinced that a limited nuclear war could be justified, the primary moral question for him was the evaluation of deterrence: the threat to use nuclear weapons.

The critical implication of this position concerns deterrence theory. Hehir is aware that the unique moral problem of nuclear weapons is not their use but the threat to use them. As he stated, "Deterrence is the hard case for policy and the limit case for the ethics of policy."[38]

Hehir identified three dimensions of the deterrence debate. The first element is the relationship between the intention to act and the execution of an act, and the moral problem is that contemporary deterrence policy is based upon a stated intention to do what a just war ethic could never legitimize—the destruction of large urban areas. The second element recognizes that an ethic of intention has to be fused with an ethic of consequences. This statement captures the moral irony of deterrence policy: the threat of nuclear retaliation, and the threat to do what would be immoral to do in fact, prevents the use of nuclear weapons. To develop the justification of this dimension, one could use the contemporary discussion based on the expanded use of the principle of proportionality and argue that there needs to be a degree of flexibility built into the decision-making process and that all factors must be assessed equally, and that in a complex situation one may use as an analytical structure "the lesser-evil or morally avoidable-unavoidable evil"[39] method of analysis. This use of proportionality seeks to weigh good effects and bad effects and then attempts to discern a method by which a critical moral tension can be maintained. A third element of the moral theory focuses on how the following are related: the intention to act, the perception of that intention by the enemy, and the possibility of that perception's causing the movement from intention to action. It is this dimension of the deterrence debate that has the potential to cause the highest degree of instability within the system, but again, from a morally ironic point of view, a higher perception of the willingness to act may indeed lead to a greater degree of stability.

Hehir would favor a position that includes tolerance for some deterrence strategies based on the recognition that the policy in fact has created a degree of stability and has actually inhibited the use of nuclear weapons. This conclusion should not be seen as an acceptance of nuclear weapons or of any avoidance of the serious problems connected with them. What concerns Hehir is having a means of conducting a public debate on the use of these weapons. To do this he uses the just war categories in a sustained and critical fashion so that he can connect with policy debates and offer a framework for their moral analysis. His orientation is both reasoned and reasonable, and he has made substantive contributions to the policy debate with respect to nuclear warfare and the just war theory, and also to the analysis of the method of the just war theory as a viable means for analyzing moral dilemmas regarding war in our contemporary situations.

## CHARLES CURRAN

Charles Curran, a priest of the diocese of Rochester, New York, and currently the Elizabeth Scurlock University Professor of Human Values at Southern Methodist University, in his teaching, writing, and leadership on a variety of issues, has helped members of the Catholic Church see and respond to a variety of problems and provided a methodological and theological basis for their response. While he has not written any major work specifically on the problem of war and peace, Curran's own orientation is important insofar as it attempts to provide a middle ground between an exclusive reliance on either violence or pacifism.

Methodologically, Curran looks at human reality in light of the five basic Christian mysteries: creation, sin, incarnation, redemption, and resurrection destiny. This orientation gives him a stable structure through which to view the complexity of situations that face us—especially with respect to public policy. It also provides some control over the kinds of responses that individuals and the Catholic Church make. Because Curran's methodology recognizes the presence of both goodness and evil in the world and accepts the tension that comes from living between the resurrection and the final coming of God's kingdom, his ethical analysis, accepting compromise and balance as it does, may not be as radical or as critical as that of others. While recognizing that moral compromise may sometimes be necessary, he argues that complex situations require complex analysis and response and that a one-sided approach may not respond to the issues in a productive way.

Curran does not reject the possibility of either war or revolution. In our world, he sees that these may be, in fact, necessary. However, having said that, he insists upon taking seriously the criterion that war indeed be the last resort and that a decision to enter into war or a violent revolution should be made only with the greatest reluctance and concern.[40] He is concerned that war is not always treated as the last resort and that the theory of just war itself has seldom been used honestly to evaluate a declaration of war by one's own country.

Curran is extremely sensitive to the moral evil of killing that occurs during war and sees this as one of the most serious ongoing ethical problems that we must attend to. He recognizes that war renders human life cheap and expendable, and simultaneously generates a love of violence, an insensitivity to and hatred of one's neighbor, and feelings of revenge and reprisal.[41] Such feelings tend to guarantee the violation of the rules of morality in the conduct of war itself and do not make the establishment of peace after a war is concluded any easier. While such possibilities, for Curran, do not eliminate the moral possibility of war, they do put more strict demands on conduct within war than other people would and place a higher degree of moral accountability on the process of declaring war.

In setting out his position on nuclear war and nuclear deterrence, Curran said:

> On the basis of discrimination I would be more hesitant to admit the morality of multimegaton weapons. On the basis of proportionality there seems to be no proportion and justification for such massive nuclear weapons with their tremendous destructive power. This argues not only against the massive nuclear weapons but especially against a great number of such stockpiled weapons.[42]

Even though this statement indicates Curran's moral difficulties with nuclear weapons and deterrence policy, his orientation toward a relationality–responsibility model that sees ethical values in relationship to one another, while not absolutizing any one value, leads him to argue that one can be opposed to nuclear weapons, or even be a nuclear pacifist, but not have to reject totally the possibility of using violence or violent resistance:

> In this imperfect world in which we live, justice and peace do not always go together. As a last resort I see the possibility of violence—more so even when it is used in a limited way by the weak against the strong, as in the case of liberation and revolution.[43]

Nonetheless, even though Curran can justify the use of violence, he is also aware of the dangers involved in accepting its use: a facile justification of violence, a romanticization of violence, and the continued danger of escalating its use.

While Curran's methodology, which accepts some form of moral compromise and justifies the possibility of the use of limited forms of violence, will not satisfy everyone, he recognizes the moral dilemmas in which people find themselves. Given this sensitivity to context, he has attempted to develop a methodology that will allow people to respond to those dilemmas in a coherent and conscientious fashion. He has attempted to build safeguards and limitations into his justification of violence, and he recognizes that the entire community—religious and civil—must be a part of the decision-making process. While Curran's methodology is tolerant of a certain amount of difference of opinion within the religious community, it provides a way for people with different values and perspectives on war and violence to begin talking with each other in an attempt to work out a common viable strategy to resolve the moral problem of war.

## GORDON ZAHN

Gordon Zahn, professor emeritus of sociology at the University of Massachusetts Boston and now living in Milwaukee, has been quite consistent in his pacifist stand for several generations now. Early in his life he became a pacifist—a position he claims was partly a consequence of not having been socialized in a traditional Catholic education system—and this led to his being a conscientious objector during World War II. Consequently, he was sent to a civilian public service camp in New Hampshire where he, along with other dissenters, was to engage in work of national significance. However, they spent most of their time attempting to clear a forest of trees that were felled during a storm.

Zahn's career took a significant turn when he matriculated at Catholic University and did both his master's and doctoral work under the direction of Paul Furfey, focusing on the experiences of the camp and the beliefs of members of the camp. In his teachings, he focused on the sociology of war and peace and has presented courses and seminars on different aspects of the peace movement. In his scholarly work, Zahn has devoted all of his energies to writing on various aspects of pacifism and its implementation in both Church and civil society. Over the past several decades, Zahn has produced a continuous stream of articles and books that explicate his position as well as critique the policies of the United States and other countries for their continued preparations for war and total destruction. Nor have the policies of the Catholic Church been exempted from this critique. In retirement, Zahn continued with some teaching, lecturing, and writing on pacifism, as well as a weekly service in a Catholic draft counseling center in Boston. He now lives in an assisted retirement community in his hometown of Milwaukee.[44]

Zahn made two major points in many of his writings. First, he holds that the stance of the early Church, that of nonviolence and pacifism, is the authentic position of the Church and ought to be reclaimed as its official position. In many ways, Zahn views the history of Christianity from about the third century, at least with respect to the question of war, as a fall from grace. Many of his writings attempt to persuade members of the Church and its leaders to return to this original position, which he perceives to be the authentic position. Second, Zahn has led a massive, critical, and substantive assault upon the just war theory, arguing that it is simply inapplicable to the modern context of war—if indeed it was ever applicable to any war. In addition to his perception that the just war theory allows a degree of moral compromise that he finds unacceptable, Zahn argues that even as a theory it is unworkable because the range of destruction envisioned by modern warfare cannot be encompassed by the theory and because the socialization of citizens is so total that they cannot step back to evaluate critically the policies of their government in terms of the methodology.

Two other interests of Zahn's continue to manifest themselves in his writings. The first focuses on the state's use of the Church to implement its political decisions. Zahn demonstrated this hypothesis in his work on the Catholic Church's role in supporting the policies of Nazi Germany in World War II by failing to denounce Hitler's agenda and by affirming a citizen's duty to obey the state. Other writings suggest that this orientation is operative in the United States and that the Church is continuously in danger of being used as a means of social control by the state in achieving its political goals. The other theme finds expression in Zahn's work on the role of individual moral decision making. Zahn has done much interesting work in terms of providing an ethical and sociological analysis of conscience and its role in moral decision making. In many ways this theme comes out of his own personal experience and the problems he encountered in acting out his conscientious decision to oppose war. It received confirmation and strength from the work that has brought him the most personal satisfaction: his work on the Austrian peasant Franz Jaegerstetter, one of the few Catholics who actively opposed the Nazis and who was executed for his acts of dissent and resistance. The example of this almost solitary Catholic dissenter to Hitler's war has proven a model of inspiration for Zahn and many other individuals as they embark on their own conscientious journeys of evaluation of the policies of different nation-states with respect to war.

Zahn has frequently been faulted for his single-mindedness and total commitment to pacifism. Many individuals have also called him to task for his linking of pacifism and abortion, based on his perception that life may not be violated at any stage or in any way. But Zahn takes his pacifism seriously and greatly values moral consistency.

Zahn has been one of the primary standard-bearers for pacifism and has offered a courageous critique of the war policy and strategy of this nation. While many do not agree with him, nonetheless many have been challenged by him and his work to examine more critically the just war theory and the policies of our country. In many ways Zahn is one of the individuals responsible for the resurgence of the viability of pacifism and nonviolence in contemporary American Catholicism. His writings certainly provided the theoretical underpinnings for such an outcome, and he himself has long been active in various movements and organizations whose work has proven to be effective in having different dimensions of Catholicism reexamine their stand on war. His continued witness to the cause of peace and his willingness to be present at demonstrations and meetings and to engage in constant dialogue with other members of the Church helped provide a vision and framework for a reevaluation of war in contemporary Catholicism. His faithfulness in promoting the cause of peace has certainly been one of the sources that the current critique of war and the promotion of peace rely on.

# 4

+

# Contemporary Developments: The State of the Question

When the Vietnam War ended and the debates, dissent, and rancor that characterized the conduct of that war subsided, the whole nation seemed to quiet down and go into a sort of moral and psychic hibernation. Perhaps the country needed a respite from the intensity and the divisions that the Vietnam War and the concomitant civil rights debate brought about in our country. Perhaps people wanted to get on with other dimensions of their lives. Student leaders were entering the job market and needed to establish themselves. Families were started and life seemed to move along. Then the Watergate scandal burst upon the political scene and began sapping the moral energies of our nation once more. The worst fears of many individuals about government surveillance and cover-ups were realized and played out in the public drama of the Watergate hearings. The issue was probably not so much the actual corruption and cover-up as it was the perception of pettiness and arrogance on the part of the individuals involved in the cover-up. The nation somehow managed to make it through the resignation of a president (Richard M. Nixon), the installation of a president (Gerald R. Ford) not elected by a national vote, and another presidential campaign without suffering the ultimate throes of despair. Another oil crisis visited itself upon our country and caused other problems. These events were heightened by the prolonged captivity of fifty American citizens held hostage by Iran from fall 1979 until January 1981. Perceptions and feelings of frustration and despair were mixed by an increasing desire to use less restrained measures to liberate the captives, but this was not to be and we awaited their release for more than 400 agonizing days.

After the perception of the aimlessness of the Carter administration in both domestic and foreign policy, the philosophy of the Reagan administration at least offered a clear alternative. Reagan may have surprised many people by following through on many of his campaign promises, especially those reducing the amount of federal monies made available for various entitlement programs and for increasing the defense budget, while simultaneously lowering taxes. However, the policies of the Reagan administration, or perhaps the dues that needed to be paid as the result of previous administrations that Reagan inherited, set the context for the debate about war and peace and the defense budget in the 1980s.

Two particular issues were important in that debate. The first was the dramatic increase of the military budget. Projections called for increasing the budget by over $1,640 billion during the Reagan presidency. These budgetary increases were accompanied by an initial hard line on foreign policy and the appearance of a willingness to use the weapons at hand if we perceived that the Soviets were stepping out of line. Whatever the exact amount of the defense appropriations enacted by the Reagan administration, the total seemed to many to be disproportionate.

The other dramatic reality involved the significance and severity of the defunding of various entitlement programs. Again, while many would feel reasonably comfortable in saying that there has been waste in these programs, nonetheless there was a perception that the Reagan administration attempted to dismantle most, if not all, of the social welfare programs of our recent past. The claim that this was done to decrease the federal budget is not quite true. What actually occurred was a massive transfer of funds from one set of accounts, the social welfare accounts, to the military account. Thus while the rhetoric was budget reduction, in effect what we experienced was the transfer of funds from one line item to another. Another major problem was the genuine hardship being caused by the decrease of funding for domestic social programs. At a time of increasing inflation and unemployment, the defunding of many entitlement programs caused enormous hardship to hundreds of thousands of individuals in our country. The price of the escalating military expenditures literally came out of the pockets of the poor.

## RESPONSES OF THE AMERICAN CATHOLIC BISHOPS

At their November 1981 meeting, the National Conference of Catholic Bishops (NCCB) established an ad hoc committee on war and peace, headed by then Archbishop Joseph Bernardin of Chicago. The committee was authorized to produce a document that would present the bishops' views on warfare today. Bernardin suggested some issues in an initial statement. First he gave a summary of the four principal contributions of the Pastoral Constitution on the Church in the Modern World, the Vatican II document also known by its Latin title *Gaudium et spes*:

First, in its assessment of scientific weapons of mass destruction, of which nuclear weapons are the principal example, the Council uttered a clear condemnation. It had condemned attacks on civilian centers and large populated areas as a crime against God and humanity (paragraph 80). Second, it supported the right of conscientious objection, a pacifist position, in the clearest statement yet in Catholic teaching. Third, it reasserted the right of nations to acts of legitimate defense, an acknowledgement that some uses of force, under restricted conditions, could be justified. Fourth, the Council raised, but did not resolve, the moral issues posed by the doctrine of nuclear deterrence.[1]

He then traced some of the related positions in recent statements of Catholic bishops. One of these was the emergence of a sort of Catholic pacifism. In addition, there was an acknowledgement of the continuing legitimacy of service in the military as service to society, as well as an endorsement of the right of conscientious objection and selective conscientious objection. Finally, Archbishop Bernardin highlighted the testimony of Cardinal Krol in 1979 to the Senate Foreign Relations Committee in which he made three interrelated moral judgments:

First, the primary moral imperative is to prevent any use of nuclear weapons under any conditions. Second, the testimony judges that the possession of nuclear weapons in our policy of deterrence cannot be justified in principle, but can be tolerated only if the deterrent framework is used to make progress on arms limitation and reduction. The third principle, a corollary of the second, is the imperative for the super powers to pursue meaningful arms limitation aimed at substantial reductions and real disarmament.[2]

These considerations led Archbishop Bernardin to set the following issues as illustrative of the concerns for the committee: First, develop a positive theology of peace that looks beyond limiting the destructive power of war. And second, examine the implications of the stringent limits placed on the use of force in our day by recent popes. This orientation will look not only at nuclear war but the nonnuclear use of force.

However, Bernardin was careful to note that the moral problem of nuclear war would be the most challenging task and probably the center of attention for the committee. He gave several reasons for this. First, the United States was the first to develop and use atomic weapons. Second, the United States is among the countries that helped develop nuclear weapons of greater accuracy and national security strategies around those weapons. Third, there has been an increasing coupling of the use of deterrence with a willingness to fight limited nuclear wars. Fourth, positions taken by American Catholic bishops over the previous decade challenged significantly the U.S. policy of defense.

How this committee would pull all of the various strands of moral reasoning together in a coherent statement was not clear at that time. Nonetheless, the fact that such a commission was established and that it would examine the significant moral questions concerning our war and deterrence policy of the day was extremely important. In many ways the process of going through such an examination of a moral position with respect to war, and especially nuclear weapons, may be more important than the actual document itself. For what this committee did, on the one hand, was to validate the questioning of U.S. foreign policy especially with respect to nuclear weapons and deterrence and, on the other hand, to recognize the validity and significance of the contributions of the Catholic peace movement of the previous several decades.

## STATEMENTS OF INDIVIDUAL BISHOPS

Several bishops made their own statements about war and peace in advance of the report by this committee. Summaries of statements from several bishops follow as a way of indicating the context in which the committee did its work.

### Bishop Anthony M. Pilla of Cleveland, Ohio

Bishop Pilla phrased his examination of the question of the morality of nuclear war within the context of traditional Christian respect for the sanctity of life and suggested this as the basis for a Catholic reevaluation of the questions raised by the awesome power of nuclear weapons. After presenting a summary of the just war theory, its applicability to traditional warfare, and a critique of the bombing of Hiroshima in 1945, Pilla then went on to raise several questions about nuclear warfare.

The majority of the positive part of Pilla's statement is a reiteration of the teachings of recent popes and the Vatican Council, as well as pastoral letters from the American bishops on nuclear warfare. The general tone and orientation of his statement is that nuclear war is very difficult to justify and that significant problems are raised both by building nuclear weapons and by using them in a policy of deterrence. What is significant about his orientation is that it picked up on a concern raised by Archbishop Bernardin: the presentation of a positive theology of peace in which the intent of Christian moral questioning and action is not simply to outlaw war, but to promote and build the structures of justice that will permit peace to flourish.

A number of positive recommendations for acting on some of the Church's teachings about war and peace concluded this statement. These included, but were not limited to, establishing a peace and justice committee in each parish, instituting an annual peace week to promote peace education in the diocese, planning liturgies for national holidays to help raise the awareness of the difference between patriotism and militarism, urging Catholics involved in the production of weapons of mass destruction to reconsider the moral implications of working in such places, supporting the establishment of a World Peace Tax Fund as an alternative to using tax monies for war, helping to train draft counselors, and supporting and participating in the nuclear freeze campaign.

Bishop Pilla concluded his statement with a very important challenge that showed how questioning the policy of the government is an act of patriotism, even if it criticizes what the government is doing:

> As the prophets criticized the immorality of the societies in which they lived, so we must unite to oppose the evils inherent in our own political system. The emphasis placed on military buildup and weapons proliferation in our country is one such evil.[3]

### Archbishop John R. Quinn of San Francisco, California

Archbishop Quinn, now retired, used the occasion of the eight hundredth anniversary of the patron saint of San Francisco to make a pastoral statement on the issue of war and peace. In his 1981 letter, he proposed St. Francis of Assisi as a prophet of poverty and peace for our own age and used this inspiration to help examine the question of the use of nuclear weapons and the escalation of the arms race.

Quinn began his statement by focusing on the moral dilemma that we face as a consequence of having developed nuclear power: we created a military technology without thinking through its moral implications, or, to rephrase it, we developed a technology without questioning whether we have the moral capacity to control the power we created. Quinn captured this dilemma by quoting Albert Einstein, who recognized that the splitting of the atom changed everything but our modes of thinking.

Quinn cited this phrase as a way of challenging Christians to rethink our nuclear strategy. He indicated that the United States has a stockpile of nuclear weapons equivalent to six hundred and fifteen thousand times the explosive force of the bomb dropped at Hiroshima. This gives the United States an overkill power of about forty. By contrast, the Soviet Union has an overkill power of about seventeen. Quinn noted that we continue to build three nuclear warheads per day and that these account for a large part of the hundreds of billions of dollars that were budgeted for the Pentagon. He also argued that this spending on weapons is a form of theft from the poor because resources that are needed for their very survival are diverted from them in preparation for war.

Quinn began his presentation of the teachings of the Church by noting two elements: (1) the statement from the Gospel of Matthew that we shall not kill and (2) a recognition that the gospel teaching does not rule out the right of nations to protect themselves against enemies. Quinn located the particular moral problem of our age as occurring when the effects of our defensive weapons are no longer fully predictable or within our control. He then said that the teaching of the Church is clear: "Nuclear weapons and the arms race must be condemned as immoral."[4] After this he applied the traditional just war principles to nuclear warfare and drew this conclusion:

> If we apply each of these traditional principles to the current international arms race, we must conclude that a "just" nuclear war is a contradiction in terms.[5]

Quinn concluded with the recognition that there will be a diversity of responses to the challenge of the morality of nuclear war within the Catholic community, and he proposed three areas in which Catholics might work together to bring some degree of moral clarity and ethical advancement to the situation. First, he invited believers to observe a monthly day of fast and abstinence as a means of petitioning an end to the arms race. He then recommended a broad-based educational program on the Church's teaching with respect to nuclear warfare throughout the archdiocese. Finally, he asked that Christians find a practical expression for their concerns in the political and social arenas. Here he presented three specific recommendations. He asked individuals to participate in the national campaign for a nuclear arms freeze. Second, he suggested that the administrators and staff of Catholic health facilities join those who are opposing the intentions of the Department of Defense to establish a "civilian-military contingency hospital system" on the premise that this system is based on the illusion that there can be an effective medical response in the case of nuclear war. Third, he requested support for developing creative proposals for converting military weapons technology to civilian productions use.

These last two recommendations were of particular importance insofar as they were suggestions that had not been made publicly by other Catholic bishops. Quinn rightly critiqued the contingency hospital system that alleged the survivability of a nuclear war. With respect to the conversion technology, Quinn recognized that we must use the creativity we have to make this transfer and must do so in a way that will enable large numbers of people to participate in it. This last recommendation should be of particular importance for Catholics who are engineers and scientists.

A unique and wonderful contribution from these individuals would be to lead the way in developing a genuine conversion technology.

## Bishop L. T. Matthiesen of Amarillo, Texas

Bishop Matthiesen made two different statements that, while not as nuanced or clearly located in the framework of the tradition as the other bishops' statements, were nonetheless interesting and significant, especially since they evaluate war and nuclear weapons from a different perspective, that of one who lived in the town in which nuclear bombs were assembled.

For example, in his testimony on the MX missile, Bishop Matthiesen argued against locating the system in Texas as follows:

> You will crisscross our farms and our ranches with highways and yet more roads; you will uproot families, hundreds and hundreds of them; you will drain our already rapidly decreasing water supply; you will bring in a boomtown atmosphere, then leave us with ghost towns; you will require us to provide services for the work crews, and then tell us you do not need us any longer.[6]

But his most critical argument was that locating the MX system in Texas would make his area a primary target and leave innocent people at the center of a target system. Bishop Matthiesen was careful to note that he did not want the system moved elsewhere. He wanted it to be eliminated entirely, for no system that guarantees the destruction of innocent men, women, and children is morally acceptable.

Thus, his critical argument against locating the MX system in Texas was simply that it would destroy personal and social life as the people knew it and would guarantee that the innocent would be placed in jeopardy.

Bishop Matthiesen also spoke on the subject of the production and stockpiling of the neutron bomb, and again his comments were not located within the tradition of the just war theory, for he approached the issue from a different and morally innovative perspective. He argued that the development of the neutron bomb reveals that the military can—and perhaps must—think in only one way: every advance by the enemy in arms technology and capability must be met with a further advance on our part. He then suggested that we turn our energies from this destructive use to the peaceful uses of nuclear energy and attempt to use it to produce food, fiber, clothing, shelter, and transportation. In a move that caused particular anguish for several people in his diocese, he proposed:

> We urge individuals involved in the production and stockpiling of nuclear bombs to consider what they are doing, to resign from such activities, and to seek employment in peaceful pursuits.[7]

While he did not mandate that individuals resign their jobs, he certainly gave the strong impression that such employment was morally inappropriate and that from his perspective it would be wrong for individuals to continue in such employment.

Such a recommendation raised another moral dimension of nuclear warfare: the responsibility civilians have to evaluate morally their employment. Most of the just war criteria focused attention on the state and the military; Matthiesen's recommendations raised the issue of what moral responsibilities civilians have as they pursue their livelihood. This question was especially difficult not only from a moral perspective but also from a practical perspective. As unemployment rates continued to rise and the military budget continued to increase dramatically, it was clear that many job opportunities would be found in defense-related plants and that many individuals would have to choose between employment that was morally problematic and no employment and, consequently, no support for their families. One solution to this problem was addressed through the establishment of the Solidarity Peace Fund, funded by the Oblates of Mary Immaculate, which helped employees who, for reasons of conscience, resigned from the Pantex plant where nuclear weapons are produced.

## Archbishop Raymond G. Hunthausen of Seattle, Washington

Archbishop Hunthausen made several significant statements with respect to nuclear weapons, especially the Trident system. Like Bishop Matthiesen of Texas, he did not use the categories of the just war as a means of articulating his moral opposition.

At the heart of Hunthausen's opposition to nuclear war was his understanding of the teaching on carrying the cross, present at the heart of the Gospel of Mark. He said that we cannot think about our call to carry the cross in abstract terms, but must think about it as a call to love God and one's neighbor in a direct way. This means that in our age, from Hunthausen's perspective, we must take up the cross of unilateral disarmament and risk living without the alleged security of nuclear weapons:

> Our security as people of faith lies not in demonic weapons which threaten all life on earth. Our security is in a loving, caring God. We must dismantle our weapons of terror and place our reliance on God.[8]

Hunthausen then discussed two dimensions of a policy of unilateral disarmament. First, he presented the moral irony that we are more terrified by talk of disarmament than we are about the risks and consequences of nuclear war. This is because nuclear arms protect privilege and exploitation, and giving them up implies relinquishing our economic power over other nations and peoples. Divesting ourselves of nuclear weapons requires a change in our economic policies, a reality attended to by few commentators. He then said "giving up the weapons would mean giving up more than our means of global terror. It would mean giving up the reason for such terror—our privileged place in the world."[9]

A second suggestion that Hunthausen made was to engage in tax resistance by withholding 50 percent of one's taxes:

> Form 1040 is the place where the Pentagon enters all of our lives and asks our unthinking cooperation with the idol of nuclear destruction. I think the teaching of Jesus tells us to render to a nuclear-armed Caesar what that Caesar deserves—tax resistance, and to begin to render to God alone that complete trust which we now give, through our tax dollars, to a demonic form of power. Some would call what I am urging "civil disobedience." I prefer to see it as obedience to God.[10]

This dramatic statement by a Catholic bishop caused a significant amount of commentary and, to say the least, raised eyebrows in some circles. This led Hunthausen to issue a second statement that clarified but reiterated his original statement. This second statement made several other significant points. First, he argued that all nuclear war is immoral because there is no conceivable proportionate reason that could justify the destruction of life and resources that such a war would entail. Then he said that since the arms race makes nuclear war inevitable, participation in it is also immoral. He therefore concluded that unilateral disarmament is the only moral position possible in our age.

In addition to this clear articulation of his moral position, Hunthausen also took this opportunity to mention four other issues that are related to his position on nuclear war and tax resistance. First, he defended his right and duty as a bishop to speak out on the concrete issues of the day as they affect Catholic morality. He suggested that statements by a bishop should be specific and attempt, to the best of that bishop's ability, to apply the gospel to daily living. Second, Hunthausen rejected the notion that because the episcopal office is a religious office, a bishop should not speak out on political issues. Third, he reiterated his suggestions about tax resistance but, more importantly, argued against those who think that it was immoral to disobey the law of the state even for a good end. He showed the relation of the tradition of civil disobedience to traditional Roman Catholic theology and argued that it is more important to be faithful to the laws of God than the laws of the state. Fourth, he argued that every nation has a moral obligation to bring about peace and disarmament and not to make itself the strongest nation on earth: "Any nation which makes as its first priority the building up of armaments and not the creative work of peace and disarmament is immoral." In another statement, Hunthausen presented further articulations of his understanding of the moral problem of nuclear war. He asserted: "A nuclear first-strike weapon is the ultimate violation of both God's law and international law." For him this was the basis on which he condemned the Trident missile. He was also helpful in unmasking some of the moral reality hidden behind descriptions of such weapon systems by the Pentagon:

> Pentagon planners have cloaked the reality of first-strike in such terms as "counterforce" and countervailing strategy, whose meaning is in fact the preemptive destruction of enemy deterrent forces together with millions of innocent people designated by strategists as "collateral civilian damage."[11]

A second comment expressed his hope that we could learn to make peace through nonviolence with the same degree of sacrifice as those who seek peace through war:

> Non-violence requires at least as much of our lives as war does. The truth is found in Jesus' non-violent teaching of the cross: to lay down our lives out of love, not while taking the lives of others but by revering them more deeply. Our reverence for life needs to deepen to that truth at the cross where the God of love calls us to give up our lives for life itself.[12]

Perhaps the depth of Hunthausen's moral concern and outrage was summarized best in his statement that "Trident is the Auschwitz of Puget Sound." While that statement is extremely provocative and probably very troubling to many people, it nonetheless represented the conclusion of a rather significant and detailed working through of a moral position on nuclear war. Finally, Hunthausen demonstrated the depth of his commitment by announcing his withholding of 50 percent of his federal tax to protest our war policy. Such a dramatic gesture, unprecedented in American Catholicism, both opened the way to a reevaluation of this nation's nuclear policies and suggested a new strategy of resistance.

### Terrence Cardinal Cooke, Archbishop of New York and Vicar of the U.S. Military Ordinariate (1921–1983)

Until his death in 1983, Terrence Cardinal Cooke held two offices: Archbishop of New York and Vicar of the U.S. Military Ordinariate. His letter to military chaplains, written just months before his death, is different from the other messages examined thus far because it is directed to a very specific audience: the Catholic chaplains in the United States armed services. This letter was motivated by two major concerns: first, many Catholic men and women in the military services asked questions with respect to the morality of war and peace, with special emphasis on nuclear weapons; second, bishops have a special obligation to present the moral teachings of the Catholic Church to help form the consciences of its members, and this letter is an attempt to do this.

In this letter, Cooke addressed two major questions: Has the Church changed its position on military service? Must a Catholic refuse to have anything at all to do with nuclear weapons?

The first question was answered very quickly and simply by reiterating the statement from the Vatican II document *The Church in the Modern World*:

> All those who enter the military service in loyalty to their country shall look upon themselves as the custodians of the security and freedom of their fellow countrymen; and when they carry out their duty properly, they are contributing to the maintenance of peace.[13]

The second question was answered in a lengthier and more nuanced fashion. Cooke used three principles to justify the participation of Catholics in areas of the armed service that involve nuclear weapons. First, he repeated the tradition of the Catholic Church that a government has the right and duty to protect its people against unjust aggression. The implication of this is that a country can develop and maintain weapon systems to try to prevent war by deterring another nation from attacking it. Second, the Church recognized that as long as we have reason to believe "that another nation would be tempted to attack us if we could not retaliate, we have the right to deter attack by making it clear that we could retaliate."[14] Cooke argued that government leaders have a moral obligation to come up with alternatives to deterrence, but as long as we are sincerely trying to work with other nations to find a better way, the Church considers the strategy of nuclear deterrence morally tolerable. Third, he then concluded that if the strategy of nuclear deterrence is morally tolerated, those who produce or are assigned to handle the weapons that make the strategy possible could do so in good conscience.

Cooke also raised questions that a nation must daily ask itself: "How much defense is enough? How much is too much?" He recognized that a nation must use its resources on behalf of all its citizens but suggested that we may not assume that reductions in defense would automatically solve problems like poverty, hunger, and disease. While recognizing the nation's obligation to provide for different needs of its citizens, Cooke concluded that there would be "little point in a nation's spending all its resources on feeding, clothing, housing and educating the poor, and on other needs, only to leave all its people defenseless if attacked."[15]

Cooke concluded his letter to the chaplains by announcing the establishment of a House of Prayer and Study for Peace. This house was designated to be supervised by officials of the Military Ordinariate, and the board of advisors will include "men and women representing a broad spectrum of occupations and disciplines." The daily activities of prayer and study will be supported and carried out by a small staff of religious and laypersons and residents in the house itself. Choosing as a theme for the house Pope Paul VI's statement "If you wish peace, defend life," the staff will attempt to pool a variety of resources and share findings about war and peace and try to encourage individuals to join in prayer that peace with justice will be a reality within our lifetime.

What is interesting about this letter from Cardinal Cooke, in comparison to some of the other statements of bishops examined above, is its fairly close reliance on the just war theory. While this is neither wrong nor inappropriate, his use of it gave a significantly different tone and feel to this document. Another important issue in this statement was how Cooke presented the question of nuclear deterrence. He moved quickly from a general affirmation of a deterrence policy to a specific policy of nuclear deterrence. While one can find support for a position of nuclear deterrence within the Church, missing in Cooke's statement was a reasoned presentation of why that occurs. The document would be more coherent if there were some elaboration of the justification process. Finally, the letter ended on a positive tone with the establishment of the House of Prayer and Study and the linking of the protection of life to other social issues, in particular the newborn, the elderly, the poor, and the hungry. Such a linking of an affirmation of the value of life to social policy was a very helpful move and may contribute to a very serious moral examination of a variety of social policies in our country.

### John Cardinal O'Connor, Archbishop of New York and Vicar of the U.S. Military Ordinariate (1920–2000)

The late Cardinal O'Connor, Cardinal Cooke's successor and a member of the committee that drafted *The Challenge of Peace*, wrote *In Defense of Life*,[16] a book that aimed to clarify the official Catholic Church teaching on the just war theory. O'Connor focused on three questions: Is it possible to conduct a just war today? Can the use of nuclear weapons ever be justified? Is conscientious objection a right, a duty, neither, or both? What is interesting about this book is not the answers to these questions but the methodology used to answer them. The answers were presented fairly succinctly. Yes, it is possible to have a just war today. If by nuclear weapons we mean strategic weapons of mass destruction, no, we may not use them. If we understand nuclear weapons to be tactical nuclear weapons or nuclear weapons not of mass destruction, the answer was that perhaps we might justify their use. Finally, O'Connor recognized that a Catholic might be a conscientious objector when circumstances warrant. However, he noted that the Church has not come down overwhelmingly on the side of the conscientious objector as the norm, with military service as an exception.

This methodology by which O'Connor arrived at these conclusions was extremely interesting but exceedingly problematic. This section will indicate several problems with the methodology that will explain many misgivings about his conclusions. First, there was a close identification of the Church with the hierarchy. It is true that the hierarchy is an extremely important part of the Roman Catholic Church, but contemporary theology, and even traditional theology, would recognize the overriding significance of those members of the Church who are not among the hierarchy.

Second, with respect to his statement of the Church's teachings, O'Connor looked mainly to papal, conciliar, and episcopal conference documents, with an occasional nod to the statements of the ordinary of a particular diocese. Again, the statements of these groups are extremely important and serve as a kind of bellwether for reading Catholic opinion about a particular topic. Nonetheless, a vast theological literature on war and peace was not alluded to in the analysis contained in the book. In fact, in a surprising statement, O'Connor observed: "Again it is worth recalling that even though nuclear weaponry has been publicly known for some thirty-five years, professional moralists have still not provided the analyses or the body of literature similar to that available in medical ethics or other fields."[17] That statement represents a lack of awareness of contemporary literature regarding the just war theory and the literature on ethical dimensions of modern warfare.

A third issue of particular importance with respect to O'Connor's methodology was his discussion of individuals he labeled as the "neo-Gnostics." These were individuals "who in their zeal to avert war and to condemn the things of war tend to convey the impression that their personal convictions, and only theirs, reflect the true teachings of Christ."[18] They supposedly claimed that a new revelation has been given to them. Whatever the Church may have taught in the past, it could not be the true Church, or the Church of true Christians, were it to tolerate war under any circumstances in the future. These neo-Gnostics did three things that troubled O'Connor. First, they urged individuals to follow their consciences regardless of mandates from civil authorities. Second, they ignored the more thoughtful advocates of peace in the courts of military planners and government decision makers. Third, they distracted society from objectively studying the totality of discernible facts, the understanding of which is essential to the formulation of a rational response to world events and perceived provocations to war.

The major problem in responding to these claims is, first, that O'Connor never identified who these people were, thus making an evaluation of his claims difficult. Second, the three reasons that O'Connor used to argue the case that these neo-Gnostics are problematic are basically ad hominem. He does not present an argument justifying the correctness of his perceptions about these individuals and their alleged stances. A third critique of his use of this particular category is that it reflected a lack of familiarity with the opinions of authors and commentators who are not members of the hierarchy.

The most critical issue in O'Connor's entire presentation came from his ecclesiology and a heavy reliance on ecclesiastical positivism. The bottom line question for O'Connor follows: Has any pope ever said that it is a sin to participate in war? The answer is obviously "no." But one has to ask whether that is the appropriate methodological question and whether that is the only norm for evaluating what is sinful in Catholic moral theory. Such an orientation overlooks major sources of wisdom within Catholic moral theology, including, but not limited to, Scripture, tradition, theological discussion, and the belief of the community in its broadest dimensions.

## THE CHALLENGE OF PEACE: GOD'S PROMISE AND OUR RESPONSE (1983)

The American Catholic bishops, collectively and individually, have frequently addressed questions related to the morality of war. Many times their statements were, or were perceived to be, supportive of the position of the government. Often the bishops took a long time to determine what seemed fairly obvious to others. And, just as frequently, the bishops were criticized for saying anything at all about political, military, or economic policies of the government. Seldom were they praised for what they said. Nonetheless, the bishops do address matters of public policy and while what they say, or what is said on their behalf, may not please everyone or anyone, they maintain their duty to address public policy and to evaluate it in light of the Catholic moral tradition.

In contrast to the more diffuse, vague, and thoroughly unsettling threats of terrorist attacks of our time, the 1970s, 1980s, and early 1990s were characterized by specific threats and war-making strategies. The United States, for example, had well over ten thousand nuclear warheads as part of bombs, on various land- or sea-based missiles, or for use on the battlefield. Combined with this were a variety of strategic discussions: *preemptive strike*: a first launch if we thought the Soviet Union was ready to attack us; *counterforce retaliation*: retaliation at the military forces of the Soviet Union if we were attacked first; *mutually assured destruction (MAD)*: preventing the Soviet Union from carrying out a second nuclear strike by developing the capacity to annihilate the Soviet Union in response to a first strike; and *flexible response in Europe*: the battlefield use of tactical nuclear weapons in the event that either Soviet or Warsaw Pact troops invaded Europe and were successful. Additionally, the first round of discussions on the Strategic Defense Initiative—the proposal to attempt to build a missile shield in space to intercept incoming missiles—was initiated. The Berlin Wall continued to be a source of tension between East and West. The Cold War continued to be a real war in all but an actual exchange of weapons—though this was occasionally done through the use of surrogate nations. The threats to peace and security were real and palpable. The times were ripe for a reconsideration of the tradition of the just war in the context of nuclear weapons, particularly in light of the implications of deterrence theory: the threat to use nuclear weapons against military forces with enormous loss of civilian life or, in the case of mutually assured destruction, to destroy a country to prevent a second launch of their nuclear weapons.

This obligation was acted on again in an examination of the morality of war, especially nuclear war and deterrence theory. Originally titled "God's Hope in a Time of Fear," the various drafts of this pastoral letter caused so much debate and so many differences of opinion that the original publication date of November 1982 was postponed until 1983. More than seven hundred pages of comments were submitted to the bishops, and comments have appeared in various journals.[19] While some felt that this delay was just another example of the bishops' avoiding hard decisions, it also showed that the bishops realized the seriousness of the issues and wanted more time to evaluate them.

The draft of the pastoral letter had its beginning at the 1980 general meeting of the American bishops. Archbishop Roach, then president of the National Conference of Catholic Bishops, responded to Bishop Head's request, as chairperson of the Social Development and World Peace Committee, that the NCCB leadership take responsibility for a discussion of the morality of war. Archbishop Roach appointed Archbishop Joseph Bernardin to chair an ad hoc committee. Four other bishops—Fulcher, Gumbleton, O'Connor, and Reilly—were appointed. The United States Catholic Conference provided staffing in the persons of J. Bryan Hehir and Edward Doherty. Representatives from the Conference of Major Superiors of Men and the Leadership Conference of Women Religious Superiors were invited to be on the committee. Bruce M. Russett, professor of political science at Yale and editor of *The Journal of Conflict Resolution*, was appointed to be the principal author, although eventually J. Brian Hehir took over this position. Three years and three drafts later, the NCCB approved *The Challenge of Peace: God's Promise and Our Response*, a tightly reasoned and closely argued 339-paragraph analysis of the status of the just war tradition in our age.

There are two major points of emphasis in the document. The first is an articulation of the just war theory. The second identifies three basic teachings.

In their discussion of the just war theory, the bishops followed the common distinction of *jus ad bellum* (rules for declaring war) and *jus in bello* (rules for the conducting of war).

The principles of *jus ad bellum* are as follows:

1. Just cause: the reason for resorting to war must be worthy, for example, to protect innocent human life or to secure basic human rights.
2. Competent authority: a competent authority, i.e., the Congress of the United States, must declare war.
3. Comparative justice: because there is no international authority, all states should recognize the limits to the cause of war and, therefore, use only appropriate and limited means to secure justice.
4. Right intention: ultimately, this must include pursuing peace and limiting violence and destruction.
5. Probability of success: the purpose of this criterion is to prevent irrational resort to force or resistance when either will be disproportionate or futile.
6. Proportionality: the damage inflicted and costs incurred by war should be proportionate to the good to be achieved.

The principles of *jus in bello* are as follows:

1. Proportionality: response to aggression must not exceed the aggression.
2. Discrimination: there should be no direct targeting of noncombatants or nonmilitary targets.[20]

Next the bishops identified three basic teachings emerging from these general principles. The first relates to nuclear weapons and civilian populations.

Under no circumstances may nuclear weapons or other instruments of mass slaughter be used for the purpose of destroying population centers or other predominantly civilian targets.[21]

The second relates to the initiation of nuclear war.

We do not perceive any situation in which the deliberate initiation of nuclear warfare, on however restricted a scale, can be morally justified. Non-nuclear attacks by another state must be resisted by other than nuclear means. Therefore a serious moral obligation exists to develop non-nuclear defensive strategies as rapidly as possible.[22]

The third teaching, more controversial and equally morally complex, speaks to so-called limited nuclear war.

> It would be possible to agree with our first two conclusions and still not be sure about retaliatory use of nuclear weapons in what is called a "limited exchange." The issue at stake is the *real* as opposed to the *theoretical* possibility of a "limited nuclear exchange."[23]

Here the bishops are responding to the ethical quagmire involved in discussing a limited nuclear exchange in which there are many unanswered questions: would information be sufficient to know what is actually happening; would communication systems exist at all; would the specific decision to limit the exchange be possible; how precise would the targeting be; and what does limited mean in terms of radioactive fallout?[24]

Essentially, the policy and strategic questions are unresolved and may in fact be irresolvable in the abstract. The bishops, therefore, drew a prudential conclusion:

> Unless these questions can be answered satisfactorily, we will continue to be highly skeptical about the real meaning of "limited." One of the criteria of the just-war tradition is a reasonable hope of success in bringing about justice and peace. We must ask whether such a reasonable hope can exist once nuclear weapons have been exchanged. The burden of proof remains on those who assert that meaningful limitation is possible.[25]

In addition to these three positions, the bishops also put the theory of deterrence to the ethical test and in doing so provided an exceptionally cogent presentation and analysis of the key technical and ethical issues involved in this complex discussion. The discussion begins with a general consideration of four background elements raised by various parties in the debate. First, since 1945, deterrence has worked at least in the sense that we have not witnessed a nuclear exchange. Second, there is a major risk of the failure of deterrence with the consequence of catastrophic results. Third, some see deterrence theory as the driving force in the ever-escalating arms race. Finally, some argue that deterrence theory is unethical because it includes the immoral intention to attack directly civilian populations.[26]

The argument of the bishops is that while there is a moral need for a theory of deterrence as part of the legitimate defense needs of a country, not all forms of deterrence are morally acceptable. "Specifically, it is not morally acceptable to intend to kill the innocent as part of a strategy of deterring nuclear war."[27] And the bishops then argued:

> A narrow adherence exclusively to the principle of noncombatant immunity as a criterion for policy is an inadequate moral posture for it ignores some

evil and unacceptable consequences. Hence, we cannot be satisfied that the assertion of an intention not to strike civilians directly, or even the most honest effort to implement that intention, by itself constitutes a "moral policy" for the use of nuclear weapons.[28]

Given the complexity of the political, strategic, and moral analysis of deterrence theory, the bishops concluded with "a strictly conditioned moral acceptance of nuclear deterrence. We cannot consider it adequate as a long-term basis for peace."[29] This conclusion led the bishops to some evaluations: a rejection of military strategies that go beyond strict deterrence and a quest for nuclear superiority, and the affirmation that nuclear deterrence should be a step on the way to progressive disarmament.[30] The bishops then stated their opposition to "weapons which are likely to be vulnerable to attack, yet also possess a 'prompt hard-target kill' capability that threatens to make the other side's retaliatory forces vulnerable"[31]; a willingness to encourage a capability that goes beyond the deterrence levels approved by the letter; and proposals that blur the difference between nuclear and conventional weapons. The bishops then set out a series of recommendations such as a variety of verifiable and bilateral agreements to contain the development and production of nuclear weapons, support for deep bilateral cuts in the arsenals of the superpowers, support for a comprehensive test ban treaty and other reduction of weapons, a removal of weapons from potential battlefields, and the strengthening of command over existing nuclear weapons to prevent their unauthorized use.[32]

While the letter neither resolved all the moral issues associated with nuclear war nor resolved the political tensions of the Cold War, it did identify peacemaking as a moral responsibility of all, not just of Christians. Second, it provided a framework of analysis that clearly identified the moral parameters of the debate as well as political and military factors that had to be included in this debate. Finally, the letter called for a greater moral accountability on the part of the entire population in policy debates, particularly those of this magnitude. Thus the letter calls the entire population to a much higher level of conscientious and moral participation in the political life of our country.

In addition to the legacy of both calling for enhanced participation in civic life as well as providing a model of such participation, there is a further important legacy of this letter for the Catholic community: its methodology. In the development of this letter, the bishops implicitly model how to construct an ethical argument and how to draw appropriate conclusions based on that argument. First, the bishops took great care to establish as clearly and carefully as possible the empirical situation of the policy debates on nuclear warfare and deterrence theory. This was done by consulting both the relevant literature and hearing testimony, oral and written, from a very broad range of experts in the field. Second, the bishops engaged in a careful review of the Scriptures and the themes they contribute to the discussion. Third, the bishops carefully examined and recontextualized the tradition of the just war theory to set out its main ethical elements. Then the bishops used these three sets of resources to engage in an ethical analysis of the various problems presented by nuclear weapons and deterrence theory. Here the bishops moved from general scriptural and ethical considerations, through an examination of the implications of the just war theory and an analysis of policy and strategic considerations, to an evaluation that led to a variety of conclusions.

This method led to a nuanced reading of the moral obligations at various levels of the analysis. Thus the bishops argued that there are universally binding norms: noncombatant immunity. There are moral norms assumed to be applicable to all: no deliberate initiation of nuclear war. But the bishops also recognized that

> When making application of these principles we realize—and we wish readers to recognize—that prudential judgments are involved based on specific circumstances that can change or which can be interpreted differently by people of good will (e.g., the treatment of "no first use"). However, the moral judgments that we make in specific cases, while not binding in conscience, are to be given serious attention and consideration by Catholics as they determine whether their moral judgments are consistent with the Gospel.[33]

To further underscore this point, the bishops then observed: "This passage acknowledges that, on some complex social questions, the Church expects a certain diversity of views even though all hold the same universal moral principles."[34]

The letter underscores both the technical and moral complexity of such argumentation while not surrendering the possibility of cogent ethical analysis that will lead to particular conclusions. What is important though is the concurrent recognition that a set of moral principles does not necessarily lead to the same moral conclusion: the church is a community of both pacifists and just warriors. This recognition of the reality of moral authority and moral argument, as well as their proper limits and particularities, is what in the last analysis gave this particular letter such authority, commending it as a model for future moral arguments in both church and political communities.

## SUMMARY

This overview of several orientations within the Catholic Church indicates both the tension and the promise of current debates on war and peace. On the one hand, some bishops are using the just war theory as a means of articulating a traditional orientation toward war and peace. On the other hand, other bishops are adopting a much more prophetic orientation and using that as a means to critique the status quo. The bishops together hold a common goal of a search for peace, but what is being demonstrated very interestingly in the Catholic Church right now is the difference of methods with respect to how one goes about achieving that goal. We next assess the new status of the examination of the question of war and peace.

# 5

+

# Recent U.S. Foreign Policy: Political and Ethical Issues

These next two chapters survey the major trends of thought regarding peace and war, particularly within Christian circles in the United States, during the twenty-year period following the 1983 publication of the U.S. Catholic bishops' *The Challenge of Peace*. We will chart the most significant developments in theological reflection on peace issues by linking each one to the world events that prompted them. This present chapter focuses on international events that have demanded foreign policy responses, particularly on the part of the United States. The next chapter focuses more squarely on church-based peace activism and scholarship.

In undertaking these topics, a central and inescapable reminder that confronts us is the sobering realization that the final decades of the twentieth century and the opening years of our new millennium have witnessed great suffering, massive disruptions, and heart-rending atrocities. While all these tragedies are deserving of attention, certain of these have provided occasions for particularly constructive thinking about perennial as well as new issues regarding peace and war.

## THE END OF THE COMMUNIST BLOC

The single most momentous development of this era, of course, was the end of the Communist bloc, symbolized by the fall of the Berlin Wall in October 1989. With stunning rapidity and remarkably little bloodshed, a tremendous series of political changes unfolded. In the span of just a few months, Germany was reunited, the Soviet Union devolved into its constituent parts, the

Eastern European nations were liberated from the grip of the Warsaw Pact, and a sizable part of the former Eastern bloc embarked on a risky transition from a centralized command economy to free-market capitalism. Pope John Paul II, who is often accorded considerable credit for hastening the demise of Communism, offered a theological interpretation of these events in his 1991 social encyclical *Centesimus Annus*. The challenge to us living in a post–Cold War world, he contended, is to build a "civilization of love" to replace the previous world of mutual terror and distrust. A simplistic triumphalism on the part of the victors, whether it takes the form of militaristic chauvinism or an uncritical brand of economic imperialism, is not acceptable. If the new situation, where it is at last possible to speak in a meaningful way of "one world," becomes a mere excuse for a renewed exploitation of the weak by the powerful, then we have squandered our opportunity to forge a new beginning. John Paul II calls for a new solidarity that will link all peoples of the world. His challenge to develop a "globalization of solidarity" that will complete the globalization of the economy remains a key question of our age.

The significance of the end of the Cold War can be interpreted in a variety of ways, hinging on the question of what a given observer foresees as replacing the formerly bipolar division of hegemony in world politics. The most irenic and utopian account of the meaning of a post-Communist world was provided by Francis Fukuyama, a former State Department official who published a famous essay, "The End of History," in the summer 1989 issue of the journal *National Interest*. Borrowing selectively from Hegel, his French interpreter Alexandre Kojève, and others, Fukuyama proposed a view of history as possessing a *telos*, or direction, beyond the ephemeral flow of events. The fall of the Berlin Wall just months after his essay appeared seems to suggest (at least to Fukuyama's satisfaction, as spelled out in his subsequent collection of essays, *The End of History and the Last Man*[1]) that humankind has arrived at a stopping point, either temporary or possibly permanent in nature. That destination is a liberal democratic society with a free-market economy, two systems whose superiority is built into the very structure of the universe. Now that we have reached that goal throughout the world (note the convenient omission of the plight of a significant percentage of the world's population), history is effectively at an end. We have reached the zenith of inevitable progress; we should expect no further evolution of human ideology, even if events themselves do not completely stand still. The greatest struggle we are likely to face, Fukuyama reasoned, is boredom, as we have nowhere further to go once we have reached the perfect system that puts an end to the tumult of history. Many reviewers berated Fukuyama for his intellectual arrogance and his propensity to belittle the ongoing struggles of millions for relief from war and desperate poverty. Suffice it to say that the flow of events in subsequent years has cast serious doubts on his interpretation of international politics after the fall of Communism.

A sharply contrasting interpretation of world politics in the post-Soviet era was forged by Samuel P. Huntington.[2] In his 1996 book *The Clash of Civilization and the Remaking of World Order*, this Harvard political scientist predicted an era of exacerbated conflicts caused by nationalism, religious fanaticism, and clashing interests around the globe. The deck of history is not stacked in favor of peace or liberal democracy; both are likely to be endangered in a new multipolar world system that features not only great diversity and pluralism but, contra Fukuyama, inevitable antagonisms and ongoing rivalries. What sets Huntington's work apart from previous Hobbesian construals of world politics is his thesis that the existence of distinct and conflicting civilizations will hold the key to global events in the future. He predicted that the evolution of global politics after the Cold War would give a new salience to ethnic identities, solidarities, and antagonisms. As people increasingly identify themselves as members of tribes, nations, ethnic groups, and cultural-religious communities, cleavages and alliances will be determined by ties of ancestry, religion, language, values, and customs. In other words, in contrast with the Cold War era when ideology, class politics, and superpower relations mattered most, global politics is being completely reconfigured along cultural lines, as what now counts most to a majority of people are ties of blood and belief, faith and family.

According to Huntington, fault lines between the world's nine or so regional civilizations will most likely be the sites of future wars. This is particularly true where the Islamic civilization rubs up against its geographical neighbors. The case of expansionist Islam is Huntington's paradigm case illustrating his claim that religion, far from standing for the values of peace and nonviolence, is at root an impetus for division and bloody fanaticism. In a section of his book titled *"La Revanche de Dieu"* (French for "the return" or "the revenge" of God), Huntington highlights the reversal of the secularization process. The resurgence of religion since about 1950 disproved the theories of those who predicted the "withering away" of faith around the world. Increasingly, religion is perceived no longer as the "opium of the people" but now as the "vitamin of the weak," for it seems to have discovered a new way to energize the economic and political aspirations of its adherents. Religious divisions will play an important role in the conflicts of the future, and will exacerbate the latent dangers of clashes fueled by Western arrogance, Islamic intolerance, and Chinese assertiveness.

Whereas Fukuyama predicted a unified and peaceful future world, Huntington painted a picture of interminable struggle ahead, a situation for which a smug and complacent West had better prepare. He stated near the middle of his seminal work: "Cold peace, cold war, trade war, quasi war, uneasy peace, troubled relations, intense rivalry, competitive coexistence, arms races: these phrases are the most probable descriptions of relations between entities from different civilizations. Trust and friendship will be rare."[3]

Most commentators find flaws or exaggerations in Huntington's work, but few dismiss his claims out of hand. Events subsequent to the publication of his ideas in the mid-1990s seem to suggest that his portrayal of an increasingly conflict-ridden world is closer to the mark than Fukuyama's theory of the end of history. Pursuers of peace will nonetheless be horrified at the prospect of a future marked by repeated clashes of civilizations and will work to ameliorate tensions through mutual understanding and cross-cultural dialogue. A Huntingtonian future of conflict may be likely, but this does not mean that it is inevitable.

## THE ROLE OF THE LONE
## SUPERPOWER: AMERICA'S PLACE IN THE WORLD

No single item will prove more decisive for the shape of the post–Cold War world than the decisions made by the world's sole remaining superpower, the United States. An important series of recurring debates during the 1990s and the early years of the twenty-first century surrounded the basic direction of American foreign policy. Precisely what stance would America assume regarding the rest of the world? According to what ideas or value commitments would it conduct its foreign policy in this new situation? Many participants in these debates drew inspiration from a seminal volume by Harvard professor Stanley Hoffman. His book *Duties Beyond Borders: On the Limits and Possibilities of Ethical International Politics*[4] stakes out tentative positions on many of the issues treated in the remainder of this chapter, including the ethics of intervention abroad, the promotion of human rights, and various hindrances to a just world order. The influence of Hoffman's work on the landscape of current opinions regarding war and peace cannot be overstated. To appreciate his importance, one need only observe how often Hoffman's thought is cited whenever normative aspects of foreign policy are treated in print.[5]

As always, American foreign policy in this new era is drawn simultaneously to two opposite poles, two tendencies that exist in tension with one another and that work together almost paradoxically to make America what it has been since World War II: the "reluctant sheriff on the world stage." At one end lies an isolationist streak that tempts us to withdraw to a considerable extent from world events, to construe our interests narrowly, and to avoid foreign entanglements that might prove costly. At the other pole lies a thoroughgoing internationalism that propels us into substantive engagement with world events, seeking out opportunities to exert constructive influence not only on behalf of the national interest, but also for democratic values and commendable causes such as human rights. Will the United States thrust its head in the sand like an ostrich overwhelmed by the dangers it perceives? Alternately, will it fancy itself the world's police officer, attempting to ride to the rescue even when it is neither invited nor justified in doing so? Each of these orientations has its merits and shortcomings, amply demonstrated by the annals of history. In this new era as never before, the very possibility of world peace hinges on how well the United States meets the challenge of balancing these conflicting tendencies in the most constructive way possible.

Many observers of U.S. actions in the world arena lament unfortunate swings of this pendulum in recent years. U.S. military interventions in Panama, Grenada, Haiti, Somalia, and elsewhere during the 1980s and 1990s suggested to many the adoption of an overly ambitious stance of policing world events and even nation-building in contexts where this was unwise at least, or counterproductive and even incendiary at times. As with earlier swings of the pendulum in this direction, a certain amount of American exceptionalism and national messianism combined with perceived commercial and strategic interests to produce this burst of interventionism. After the turn of the millennium, particularly with the presidency of George W. Bush, the United States briefly experienced a change in the direction of the pendulum, this time toward the position of a conservative isolationism that many criticized when they observed its expressions in an irresponsible unilateralism. Evidence of this shift may be found in the U.S. rejection of the Kyoto Protocol on climate change in 2001 and the decisions in 2002 not to extend the antiballistic missile treaty with Russia nor to ratify the 1998 "Rome Statute" to establish credible prosecution of war crimes and crimes against humanity at the International Criminal Court, intended to serve as an arena of last resort for justice in cases of genocide and other atrocities. As argued on editorial pages and in scholarly foreign policy journals at the time, each of these decisions represents a retreat from a constructive internationalism and ultimately a barrier to the cause of world peace. The United States seemed to be reneging on the very commitments that would establish it as an exemplary world citizen, eager to participate in institutions critical to world order. Defenders of these decisions usually cited practical considerations, enlisting the language of national interest and pointing to feared disproportionate burdens that would fall upon the United States and American-based corporations if these agreements were ever universally enforced.

The terrorist attacks of 11 September 2001 challenged the Bush administration (and indeed all Americans) to rethink its approach to foreign policy and to renew alliances and coalitions that would enhance mutual security around the globe. Unfortunately, at least in the short term, the most tangible U.S. policy reactions to terrorism have consisted of major military budget increases (the 2003 military budget represents a 12 percent increase and is the first budget ever to approach $400 billion, which is more than the next sixteen highest military budgets of world powers combined), the establishment of a new cabinet-level Department of Homeland Security, and a sharp restriction of immigration. All of these measures suggest a turn not toward international cooperation but toward even more pronounced unilateralist entrenchment. It is not a promising sign for peace when the last remaining superpower responds to crises by seeking to establish nothing more creative than even greater military superiority.

These judgments were expressed widely in the mainstream press in the months after the 11 September 2001 terrorist attacks. Interestingly, the underlying rationale for these criticisms had previously been expressed in a 1988 publication of the National Conference of Catholic Bishops. After President Reagan in 1983 had proposed (and even procured initial funding for research into) the Strategic Defense Initiative (SDI), the bishops appointed their "Ad Hoc Committee on the Moral Evaluation of Deterrence." Over five years (1983–88), this group of seven bishops and their advisors heard testimony from over two dozen top military experts and compared the stated goals and strategies of the "Star Wars" program (as it was invariably referred to in popular parlance) to the principles and moral norms enunciated in the 1983 document *The Challenge of Peace*. The bishops recognized the vital importance of evaluating the SDI proposal, as it would fundamentally change nuclear policy, affecting virtually all issues of defense and arms control. It would also, if fully developed and employed, constitute the single most expensive military or civilian project in world history. In the summary report, the bishops' committee asked: "Are the costs of SDI justifiable in light of its likely effectiveness, probable consequences and other unmet human and military needs?" They answered: "While some of the officially stated objectives of the SDI program correspond to important themes of the 1983 pastoral on war and peace, proposals to press its deployment do not measure up to key moral criteria."[6] As always, the bishops affirmed that even this, a conclusion representing their best judgment about how universal moral principles apply in this case, leaves room for people of good will to disagree. Like all prudential judgments, it is not absolutely binding on the consciences of believers. But many found the bishops' argumentation persuasive and even cited it when the SDI was from time to time revived, proposed, and even partially funded in subsequent years.

Testing on elements of a scaled-down SDI (namely, the interception of long-range ballistic missiles, in the hopes of establishing a National Missile Shield) continue up to the time of this writing. However, with the break-up of the Soviet Union and the scaling down of Russia's military power, the actual strategic objective of deploying a nuclear shield seems far less urgent than it did at the height of the Cold War. More significant is the underlying mentality of "America going it alone," of which Star Wars is emblematic. To many observers, both at home and abroad, America's national infatuation with high-tech missile defenses is a disturbing sign. The illusion of creating an impenetrable barrier to shield American soil from all potential threats is a dangerous one, for it has the potential to feed our unilateralist impulses at a time when a constructive U.S. presence in international affairs and institutions is more essential than ever. While the sobering events of 11 September 2001 prompted many voices to declare that the United States could no longer fail to recognize its global responsibilities, we still await definitive proof that this message of constructive international engagement has filtered up to the levels occupied by the architects of U.S. foreign policy.

## THE SUCCESSION OF FOREIGN POLICY DOCTRINES

The previous section may suggest to those eager for peace and justice that the major obstacle to a more peaceful world is merely an imperial hubris grounded in America's current military superiority. However, it is also important to consider the intellectual foundations that undergird the response of the foreign policy elites in Washington. Ever since the days of Washington's Farewell Address (1796) and the Monroe Doctrine (1823), certain high-profile summaries of foreign policy wisdom have captured the collective American imagination and provided the rationale for diplomatic and military initiatives. The twentieth century witnessed new doctrines customized to the challenges faced by each generation. American foreign policy followed the wisdom offered by presidents (for example, the Truman and Nixon doctrines), diplomats (including Jeanne Kirkpatrick's distinction between authoritarian and totalitarian dictatorships, and statesman George F. Kennan's famous doctrine of containment of Soviet Communism), and other influential thinkers. Such doctrines are ordinarily subjected to ethical critique, particularly by those more committed to the cause of peace than to national interest narrowly understood. Let us take a brief look at some of the most recent doctrines that have guided American foreign policy and assess them from the perspective of an interest in peacemaking.

### The Bush Doctrine and the Conflict with Iraq (2002–03)

The most recent doctrine to consider is the Bush Doctrine. It was first publicly articulated in a 1 June 2002 speech at West Point when President

George W. Bush declared: "Our security will require all Americans . . . to be ready for preemptive action when necessary to defend our liberty and to defend our lives." Obviously, Bush was proposing his own preferred model for how to respond to terrorism. It is hardly surprising that an American president would express firm resolve in the face of such threats to the nation's security. What is novel in Bush's formulation is the jettisoning of the principle that America would not strike first, a bedrock of the Cold War strategies of containment and deterrence as well as a traditional just war principle. Bush was setting the United States on a path that might very well include unilateral preemptive action, an initiative that replaced America's customary policy of preferring to work with coalitions of allies through multilateral cooperation. Bush's immediate predecessor, President Bill Clinton, particularly insisted on gathering around his initiatives the broadest possible coalition of allies, a cue he took in turn from his predecessor George H. W. Bush, the father of George W. Bush. While the U.S. efforts in the Persian Gulf War of 1990–91 and in the series of Balkan crises in the 1990s were assisted and legitimized precisely because of the participation of so many allies, the new millennium witnessed an administration that placed a lower premium on the benefits of working within the complex network of multilateral institutions such as NATO (North Atlantic Treaty Organization), SEATO (Southeast Asian Treaty Organization), OAS (Organization of American States), and the United Nations.

We have already seen the arguments against the "go it alone" position that American foreign policy has adopted. Such a stance could backfire by stirring up resentments among other nations and by setting dangerous precedents that will serve only to embolden future hegemonic powers looking for excuses for their own expansionist aims. It could undermine the concept of national sovereignty, suggesting that any power strong enough to intervene beyond its borders could and should be able to get away with such incursions—in other words, supporting the inference that power is self-authenticating, for "might makes right." On a technical level, Bush's "fighting words" amount to a repudiation of Article 51 of the Charter of the United Nations, a statement of principles that, in addressing the topic of self-defense, leaves no room for preemptive attacks.

It is no secret that what Bush had in mind in issuing his doctrine was the justification for a future war against Iraq. Subsequent calls for a regime change that would topple Saddam Hussein confirmed this interpretation of his thinly veiled "code language." Bush had already labeled Iraq as one of three legs (the other two being the less threatening nations of Iran and North Korea) of "an axis of evil" that supported and harbored terrorists. While the elder Bush was able to assemble a broad international coalition to counter the incursion of Saddam Hussein into Kuwait and to launch the multilateral Desert Shield and Desert Storm Operations during the Gulf War a decade earlier, international support for continuing the struggle against Iraq had practically dried up. Years of harsh economic sanctions against Iraq (which caused protracted suffering on the part of civilians and hundreds of thousands of infant deaths due to a brutal policy of economic siege) and repeated episodes of weapons inspection stand-offs had caused much of the international community to lose stomach for further actions against Iraq.

While it is true that, to many observers, Iraq's spotty record of compliance with the no-fly zones and repeated U.N. Security Council disarmament resolutions meant it probably had something to hide, perhaps chemical or biological weapons, proof of such violations remained elusive. Hans Blix and his team of U.N. weapons inspectors found little evidence to substantiate suspicions that Iraq possessed weapons of mass destruction, despite a renewed round of inspections in 2002. As the international showdown dragged on, the influence of Defense Secretary Donald Rumsfeld, Deputy Secretary of Defense Paul Wolfowitz, National Security Advisor Condoleeza Rice, and other hawks within the Bush administration eclipsed more cautious voices like that of Secretary of State Colin Powell and his deputy Richard Armitage. In a 12 September 2002 address to the United Nations, Bush signaled his determination, unless Hussein quickly disarmed, to launch a massive offensive to unseat Saddam and finish the job his father did not complete in 1991, regardless of the level of international consensus and support. In mid-October 2002, both houses of Congress passed a resolution authorizing the use of force against Iraq.[7]

By the time U.S. bombers started launching tomahawk cruise missiles on Baghdad on the night of 19 March 2003, many observers had already posed probing questions about the true motivation of the Bush administration's stance toward Iraq. Ostensibly, the push toward war had started within the context of the international community's effort for the containment of a potential threat from Iraq. When the Security Council of the United Nations unanimously passed Resolution 1441 in November 2002, it looked as if the United States was simply spearheading a worldwide effort to pressure Iraq into compliance with weapons controls, a reasonable measure for collective security. However, subsequent events demonstrated a disturbing disregard for world opinion. When Germany, France, and Russia expressed displeasure with heightened U.S. rhetoric, Secretary of Defense Rumsfeld dismissed them as part of a moribund "old Europe" that was irrelevant to global challenges like the Iraq situation. It is little wonder that when war did break out, support for what Bush called "the coalition of the willing" was reduced to three dozen countries, fewer than one-fifth of the international community. Most of these countries were small and unwilling or unable to commit resources to the war effort. The fighting was left to the armed forces of the United States, the United

Kingdom, and Australia, with some minimal logistical and financial assistance from Spain, Italy, and Poland.

The relative isolation of the United States in its endeavor against Iraq can be explained in a number of ways. It is probably unfair to give much credence to the opinions, widely repeated in the world press at the time, that Bush was acting out of a simple desire for control of oil supplies or for revenge against an enemy that had humiliated and even threatened the life of his father. But it may be illuminating to consider the larger issue of Bush's motivation. There was more than a grain of truth behind public perception around the world that portrayed Bush as something other than a reluctant warrior in this path to war. Rather, because the Bush agenda was broader than the simple pursuit of Iraqi disarmament, American participation in the prolonged diplomatic dance at the United Nations was a bit of a charade. If Bush seemed overly eager to assert American power in the Middle East, it can be explained as a function of an underlying commitment on the part of his top foreign policy advisors to a distinctive and radical vision of America's place in the new world order.

Fortunately, attributing motives to the chief architects of U.S. foreign policy in the new millennium is not a matter of guesswork, but simply one of public record. Periodically, the executive branch of American government publishes a document explaining the objectives and strategies of its foreign policy. In September 2002, the Bush administration released the thirty-three–page document titled *National Security Strategy of the United States of America*. The *New York Times* called it "the first comprehensive rationale for shifting American military strategy toward preemptive action against hostile states and terrorist groups developing weapons of mass destruction."[8] Going far beyond a statement of national resolve to defeat terrorism, the document asserted this intention: "Our forces will be strong enough to dissuade potential adversaries from pursuing military build-up in hopes of surpassing or equaling the power of the United States."[9] This new and radical commitment to American global dominance explains Bush's insistence on the language of regime change in Iraq, while the rest of the world community spoke merely of containing a weapons threat. In seeming contradiction of its campaign platform and its proclivity in its early months for near isolationism, the Bush administration seemed to have come into office with an "Iraq project" already in mind. Using Iraq as a key example of the need for action, this plan called for an enhanced assertion of U.S. power wherever a threat was perceived. Especially after 11 September 2001, the Bush Doctrine would not settle for mere containment, even in cases where the threat to American lives or interests remained unproven.

Ethical critiques of this new articulation of a muscular foreign policy appeared immediately. Within weeks, one *Washington Post* columnist labeled the Bush Doctrine of preemptive war "a new imperialism" and "a re-imaging of the American role in the world" that "is like an armed evangelism."[10] A *New York Times* op-ed called it "a grand project," "a new crusade" in which "America means to remake the world, . . . to go abroad in search of monsters to destroy."[11] Jim Hug, S.J., president of the Center of Concern, a Washington-based advocacy center for global justice issues, rejected it as "a betrayal of the American spirit." He explained that the document is full of "distorted definitions, the trivialization of our national values, inconsistencies between rhetoric and recent U.S. actions, internal contradictions and disturbing silence about the historically proven need for institutional checks and balances."[12] Hug joins many other ethicists who find the document dangerous because it projects a vision of desirable world order in which no aggressive behavior on the part of a hegemonic United States is out of bounds. The need for security becomes an excuse for almost any course of action; necessity comes to justify global domination without regard for self-control.

The categories of the just war theory played a prominent role in the arguments of both hawks and doves on the Iraq question during 2002–03. "Hawks" tended to turn the just war theory on its head, reversing the key criteria that foster restraint and that reflect the Christian presumption against the use of force.[13] Besides undermining the distinction between acts of self-defense (the only type justified by the just war theory and international law) and wars of aggression, the logic of a preemptive strike depends on a psychological process of utterly demonizing one's target. In the case of Iraq, it became a matter of portraying Saddam Hussein as not only possessing weapons of mass destruction but also fully intending to use them —not only against internal dissident groups or his immediate neighbors but also (in a claim that contradicts the raw facts of the case) against the United States itself. In the face of such an imagined threat, according to the logic of the hawks, no moral principles beyond sheer national interest should be applied to proposed courses of military action, no matter how massive the violence they will unleash.

Those opposed to a direct and unilateral attack on Iraq (a grouping of "doves" that included such unusual voices for restraint as arms negotiator Brent Scowcroft and former Secretaries of State James A. Baker III, Lawrence Eagleburger, and Henry Kissinger, as well as the more expected voice of former President Jimmy Carter[14]) resisted the clamor for war with a variety of arguments borrowed from the just war theory. The search for creative and multilateral ways of containing Saddam Hussein, they argued, should continue without a premature resort to military strikes. Ironically, many argued that the only way to ensure that Iraq would indeed attempt to use its suspected stockpiles of chemical and biological weapons would be to launch a full-scale invasion of its territory. The costs of a military attack would extend far beyond the casualties on both sides, and would include the dangers of prolonged destabilization of an already chaotic Iraq, a regional escalation of hostilities, and even the potential collapse of the fragile coalition against terrorism. Other casualties of a strike against Iraq would be respect for key principles of international law such as territorial sovereignty and national self-determination. Without these limits, the ascendancy of Bush's proposed doctrine of preemptive war would set a precedent for unilateral interventions that would isolate the United States in the arena of diplomacy. America would be perceived more than ever as a "cowboy vigilante" intent on exerting its will in arbitrary ways. In fact, Vice President Richard Cheney openly used "Old West" frontier metaphors during the Iraq crisis, and observers criticized both the style and substance of his administration's foreign policy, one that threatened to render the world a far more dangerous and less predictable environment.

Bush's rush to war received immediate criticism, much of it along the lines sketched previously. The new unilateralism in American foreign policy seemed especially foolhardy because it was couched in the Manichean terms Bush employed in both prepared and off-the-cuff statements: "If you're not with us, you're against us"; "No country that cooperates with terrorists can work with the United States"; and "When it comes to our security, we really don't need anybody's permission." Many editorialists and foreign policy commentators pointed out how this approach fails to recognize the "shades of gray" that will prove crucial to the success of U.S. goals. Indeed, the most successful antiterrorist program would "make a few strange bedfellows" for the United States, including such strategically located nations as the inscrutable Syria and the jittery and seriously divided Pakistan.

Many of the most perceptive insights about these matters came from the pens of those who were familiar with the work of Joseph S. Nye, Jr., particularly his book *The Paradox of American Power: Why the World's Only Superpower Can't Go It Alone.*[15] Nye, the dean of Harvard's Kennedy School of Government, argued that American military superiority need not necessarily provoke resentment that will give rise to challenges around the globe. If properly managed (Nye used the historical example of the benevolent hegemony of Britain in the nineteenth century), the power of leading nations can be perceived as protecting universally enjoyed freedoms, benefits, and a host of global public goods. The implication is that it is dangerous to walk down the path Bush had opened, one that in principle is willing to turn its back on the network of multilateral institutions and agreements in favor of narrowly defined national interests. An inadequate analysis of power relations by American foreign policy-makers, culminating in the Bush Doctrine, had reached the wrong conclusion. Whereas most of the world (including America's traditional allies) was looking to U.S. leadership to usher the world to a stable multipolar political system that would succeed the uneasy bipolar stand-off of forty-five years of Cold War, Bush was holding out an unattractive future characterized by a permanently unipolar world led by a muscular and hectoring American hyper-power.

In the months after the 2003 war with Iraq, observers were left with more questions than answers. To what extent would the successful three-week military campaign to unseat the regime of Saddam Hussein be perceived as a validation of the doctrine of preemptive strikes? If the victory in Iraq is indeed viewed as a template for future interventions, in what corners of the globe and under what circumstances will American military force next be unleashed? Will the United States dare again to cite the pretext of eliminating weapons of mass destruction (which proved so thoroughly elusive after the fall of Saddam Hussein's government) in future assertions of military power?

Further questions abound regarding the legacy of this conflict and the buildup to it. Since America displayed its willingness to resort to near unilateralism, has permanent damage been done to major international security institutions like the United Nations? How badly will the Bush administration's willingness to stretch the truth and to cite dubious intelligence sources to build its case for Operation Iraqi Freedom injure the future credibility of American leaders? And what lessons would be drawn from the painstakingly slow process of restoring rule over that shattered country to the Iraqis themselves? Or from the necessity to retain in Iraq 150,000 American troops, who too often became targets for sniper attacks and ambushes, in order to occupy and pacify the country for months after the liberation of Iraq and the ostensible triumph of American might?

Above all, how would the war be remembered? Would we selectively recall only the glorious photo opportunities of statues of dictators tumbling to dusty plazas and of a victorious commander-in-chief landing aboard an offshore aircraft carrier? Or would we remember the 320 deaths of British and American soldiers who lost their lives in Iraq in the first five months after the 19 March 2003 invasion? Would there be any place in our collective memory for the several thousand documented Iraqi civilian casualties of the war, much less the uncounted tens of thousands of Iraqi soldiers killed before the 1 May 2003 declaration of an end to major combat operations? On the issue of how we remember and draw lessons from this conflict will hinge the future of how America uses its unprecedented global dominance and whether it can resist the imperial temptation it faces.

## The Clinton and Powell Doctrines (1990s)

The Bush Doctrine, with its proclivity to justify an expansive view of the desirability of American intervention abroad, succeeded two doctrines that had been articulated in the 1990s for the express purpose of limiting U.S. interventions. The first was the Clinton Doctrine, not so much a formal statement as an operational principle distilled by observers of the foreign policy enacted during the Clinton administration. It stated that the United States would intervene abroad only when U.S. casualties were guaranteed to be minimal. Clinton's approach was perhaps best summarized by his remark on 25 May 1994 at the Naval Academy graduation ceremony: "We cannot turn away from [ethnic trouble spots around the world], but our interests are not sufficiently at stake in so many of them to justify a commitment of our folks." This doctrine demonstrated an appropriation of the lessons of Vietnam, when an unpopular war grew even more divisive as the number of American soldiers coming home maimed or in body bags grew.

A corollary of the Clinton Doctrine stated a preference, when conflict was inevitable, for air wars, where the rules of engagement could be strictly enforced and controlled and where it was possible to avoid the deployment of ground troops vulnerable to horrific losses (as the United States experienced when 241 U.S. Marines were killed in their barracks by a car bomb in Lebanon in 1983). These preferences for the form of last-resort interventions matched Clinton's predilection for multilateralism, allowing the United States to define its contribution to joint operations, since the U.S. Air Force remained second to none. U.S. diplomacy during the Clinton era also exhibited "a nose for the soft forces" that tend to influence the outcome of conflicts more than is usually acknowledged, including nonmilitary considerations such as pressures exerted by NGOs and historical, religious, and even ethnic relationships that often play a role in negotiations and the outcomes of conflicts.

General Colin Powell had been a key player in the Gulf War and maintained his visibility as perhaps the most widely respected Republican during the Clinton years. Tapped in 2001 to be Bush's Secretary of State, he had earned a reputation for caution and even extreme risk-aversion regarding deployments of U.S. troops. The much-debated Powell Doctrine stipulated that the military should never go into combat without three things: (1) a clearly defined goal, (2) the necessary resources, and (3) an exit strategy. If any of these three elements was lacking, adherents to this doctrine recommended that U.S. forces not be deployed. The Powell Doctrine overlapped in obvious ways with the Clinton Doctrine, and their combined influence during the 1990s shaped U.S. responses to a series of international crises. Some of these involved humanitarian crises and genocides, others the chaos generated by regional ethnic conflicts, drug wars, failed states, rogue states, and the break-up of existing nations or attempts at secession. As American policy-makers weighed the risks and potential benefits of numerous proposed interventions in that particularly eventful (indeed, harrowing) decade, these were among the key ideas that drove their analysis.

## DEBATES OVER THE LEGITIMACY OF INTERVENTIONS

### The Balkan Conflicts of the 1990s

The most protracted conflict of the 1990s involved the break-up of Yugoslavia. The Serbian political leadership (including the ruthless Slobodan Milosevic) that controlled the apparatus of the central government in Belgrade attempted to prevent the secession of the constituent parts of the multi-ethnic republic, which had been artificially held together by Marshall Tito and his successors for five decades. Slovenia and Croatia slipped away relatively quickly in the early 1990s, but massive bloodshed and repression soon visited the multi-ethnic region of Bosnia and Herzegovina, where ethnic Serbs (Orthodox Christians), Croats (Roman Catholics), and Bosnians (Muslims) who had lived side by side for centuries were suddenly locked in mortal combat for the control of key slices of Bosnia's territory. The once splendid city of Sarajevo found itself one of the chief battlegrounds, much of the city lying in utter ruins or else cut off from the airport (and hence the outside world) by snipers' alleys that just a few years earlier had been peaceful roads over which had passed the Olympic torch. Evidence of atrocities on the part of all parties to the conflict surfaced gradually. We now know that 250,000 died during these conflicts from 1992 to 1995, and an additional two million people were displaced from their homes. A particularly bloody campaign of ethnic cleansing and systematic murder and rape by Serbian forces (both from Belgrade and local Bosnian Serb militias) reached the eyes and ears of international audiences by 1994. For many months, the international community dithered in indecision, unable to muster the resolve to act. Eventually, American air power, accompanied by allied ground troops and United Nations peacekeeping forces, was deployed and managed to stabilize the situation until diplomacy could succeed in reaching a workable compromise. The Dayton Accords of 21 November 1995 divided Bosnia into spheres of influence controlled by the various parties to the ethnic conflict. This remains an uneasy peace in a region that has historically been Europe's most volatile tinderbox.

Another Balkan imbroglio, the Kosovo crisis of 1999, was ignited by news reports (later largely confirmed when mass graves were discovered) of a purge of the Kosovars, an ethnic Albanian people who had come to be the largest demographic group occupying the semi-autonomous extreme southern region of what was left of the Serb-dominated Republic of

Yugoslavia. The Kosovo Liberation Army had prompted this Serbian crackdown and brutality by stepping up their demands for greater independence or union with adjacent Albania. In a poignant example of missed opportunities for maintaining peace, KLA militancy and guerrilla tactics against the Serb overlords gained local support only after fledgling nonviolent movements for the liberation of Kosovo were met with indifference from the outside world, including NATO and U.S. stakeholders in the region. As hundreds of thousands of Kosovars fled their farms and towns as refugees, tricky questions arose about the very nature of this crisis. Was it best characterized as an internal issue, a struggle for self-determination within the sovereign state of Yugoslavia? If so, would external actors, such as NATO, to whom the Kosovars appealed for assistance, be within their rights to intervene for the cause of self-determination of this threatened ethnic minority? And even if just cause and feasibility could be established, which agent (the United States, the United Nations, NATO, or the European Union) was the appropriate one for such an intervention? What type of force could be justified—relatively risk-free air strikes alone or the more precise but likely costly use of ground troops? What limits (of time, extent, and mode of deployment) were to be observed or imposed? As it turned out, a resolute display of NATO air power against Serb positions (both within Kosovo and even deadly bombing raids against targets in the Yugoslav capital of Belgrade) over the course of a few weeks in the summer of 1999 settled the situation and forced the Serbians into retreat, paving the way for hammering out a diplomatic agreement on the future of Kosovo. Yet these questions about the legitimate use of force lingered alongside the uneasy settlement.

### Genocide and the Politics of Rescue: Rwanda and Beyond

The mention of ethnic cleansing in the former Yugoslavia raises a key issue regarding humanitarian intervention: the specter of genocide. The twentieth century amply deserves the tragic title "the century of genocide" for a series of unspeakable atrocities it witnessed: Turks slaughtering Armenians, Pol Pot systematically decimating the population of Cambodia, and the paradigmatic case of the Jewish Holocaust at the hands of Nazi perpetrators. The most egregious genocide of the past twenty years unfolded during one hundred bloody days in the spring of 1994 in Rwanda, where members of the Hutu tribe massacred eight hundred thousand people, mostly rival Tutsi tribespeople as well as many Hutu moderates. Many of the slaughtered were brutally hacked to death by machetes and knives, and no segment of the Tutsi population was spared. As the scope of the calamity was revealed in the following months, (mostly) Western observers were engaging in tormented soul-searching about their role as guilty bystanders. How could we have allowed this cataclysm to unravel before our eyes? What prevented us, as nations and as the international community as a whole, from acting to prevent it or at least stop it in mid-course?

The literature that has appeared since the Rwandan genocide underlines the claim that the right or duty to intervene is never so clear. Even when the outside party is acting in a disinterested way, in pursuit of universal standards such as human rights, it is still a matter of controversy to cross a border even in a situation of rescue. After all, the principle of nonintervention is the *prima facie* norm in international law, and exceptions to this norm must be rigorously justified. Compounding the problem is the reluctance to label as genocide systematic atrocities like the one in Rwanda, even when all the elements are present, because the mere use of the "g-word" triggers an obligation to intervene, as written in the 1948 Genocide Convention.

One of the most forthright figures to expose the defects of such inherited patterns of thinking on humanitarian intervention and genocide is Samantha Power, the author of the chilling book *"A Problem from Hell": America and the Age of Genocide*.[16] Power condemns America's "consistent policy of nonintervention in the face of genocide" and documents the failure of any American administration to make genocide prevention a priority. She posits a duty to intervene whenever large numbers of civilian lives are threatened, and is not afraid to identify a range of actors (superpowers, neighboring powers, international institutions) upon whom this solemn duty falls. The tone of urgency in her writings is intended to overcome the legacy of deliberate indifference in the face of mass suffering, but her critics have targeted as naive her appeals to "the conscience of humanity" and her assumption that the justification for future interventions will be obvious to all rather than appearing to be a "smokescreen" or "fig leaf" for expansionist powers.

Michael Ignatieff, Power's colleague at the human rights program at Harvard's Kennedy School of Government, is another perceptive observer of issues related to genocide and humanitarian interventions. He shares Power's conclusions about the imperative to act against human rights violations and in his voluminous writings draws richly upon his decades as a journalist and freelance intellectual. Ignatieff is a rigorous thinker whose writings are difficult to categorize since he brings the tools of an intellectual historian, an ethicist, and a reporter to contemporary issues. In books such as *The Warrior's Honor: Ethnic War and the Modern Conscience*,[17] *Human Rights as Politics and Idolatry*,[18] and *Virtual War: Kosovo and Beyond*,[19] he treats topics he has experienced firsthand: the phenomenon of ethnic hatred and wars based on historical and cultural rivalry. His policy prescriptions always take into consideration the complexity of world events and the constraints on various actors, but consistently call upon the Western democracies to do more to prevent atrocities such as genocide and human rights abuses throughout the world.

Ultimately, Ignatieff advocates a renewal of foreign policy based more squarely than ever on human rights and the establishment of a global order to protect vulnerable people. He makes no pretense that human rights work can be seen as a matter of apolitical humanitarian rescue; in our new millennium it must inevitably proceed as an intensely political endeavor, engaging in calculated struggles for improving the entire international system. We have much hard work before us if we wish to establish the right to intervene against murderous regimes. The burden of proof remains against those who claim exceptions to the notion of absolute national sovereignty and who seek to cross borders, no matter how lofty and noble the cause. Although Ignatieff is a secular thinker, his appeals to notions like human rights and moral responsibility give his arguments a grounding in transcendent values that is persuasive to many religious social ethicists. He joins his voice to many religious leaders who call for human rights to play a more prominent role as the basis of the foreign policy of the world's great powers.

## The Issue of Nation-Building and the Somali Intervention

One frequently neuralgic point within arguments like those proposed by Power and Ignatieff involves the notion of nation-building. Although it need not be so, the term is usually employed in a derogatory way, to discredit a given proposal for sustained intervention abroad by criticizing it as overly ambitious and unrealistic. This item surfaced in the 2000 presidential debates between Al Gore and George W. Bush, with both candidates foreswearing any intention of engaging in nation-building under any circumstance. If massive U.S. efforts to promote progress toward democracy and stability did not work in Vietnam in the 1960s, the reasoning goes, why should we expect success for more modest efforts today? As the opposing argument in support of nation-building runs, the only way to truly ensure the protection of human rights and material progress in a given country or region is to invest heavily in the establishment of local institutions that will promote the health of civil society, grassroots structures that foster values like civic participation, and broad educational availability. The prospect of such deep involvement in the long-term welfare of another nation often scares away casual well-wishers, who fear the inability to sustain such a commitment.

Proposals for America to engage in a program of nation-building surfaced several times in recent years, such as in Panama and Haiti following U.S. military interventions in each country. But the paradigm case of this dynamic in debates about the wisdom of nation-building is Somalia, one of the most egregious among the many failed states around the world. These are nations in which the central government barely functions at all, or at least fails to exert adequate control to avoid the situation of utter chaos in much of its territory. Other examples include Colombia, Angola, Congo, Afghanistan, and several other of the world's poorest nation-states, which at various points in recent decades nearly succumbed to civil strife, coups d'état, rebel militias, and general disorganization.

U.S. involvement in the region of the Horn of Africa goes back to the height of the Cold War, when the Soviets and Americans courted the governments of such nations as Ethiopia, Uganda, and Sudan in order to gain strategic advantages such as access to rare minerals, vital shipping lanes, and deepwater ports. For many years, U.S. agencies tried to assist Somalia in improving its physical and social infrastructure, with little real progress to show for expensive efforts. In addition, ever since 1980, Somalia and its neighbors in northern and eastern Africa have been experiencing severe droughts. International efforts to supply emergency food relief were periodically impeded by Somali warlords who controlled large swaths of territory that blocked the flow of food inland from Somali ports. The humanitarian effort sporadically became a military mission, as U.S. forces were called upon, especially in the early 1990s, to rectify the situation to prevent mass starvation in the entire Sahel region.

Somalia is usually cited as a case that offers a cautionary tale about how interventions can backfire. What a majority of Americans probably remember most about Somalia is video footage of an October 1993 incident when eighteen U.S. soldiers were gunned down by local militias, some of their corpses dragged through the streets of Mogadishu by teenage recruits of the warlord Muhammad Farad Aided. The motion picture *Black Hawk Down*, released in 2001, captured the horror of this ghastly incident most poignantly. Although this comes as small consolation for the loss of the soldiers killed in that operation or the dozens of other U.S. casualties, to say nothing of the many thousands of Somalis on all sides whose lives were lost or disrupted by years of civil strife and famine, it is nevertheless possible to discern another brighter side of the story of this American intervention. It is often forgotten that hundreds of thousands of Somali lives were saved precisely because of American efforts to open supply lines for emergency food assistance. The forestallment of preventable starvation remains a noble goal and, arguably, a moral duty for great powers, regardless of the risks and sacrifices involved.

Despite the perception that the mission in Somalia was nothing but a costly defeat, we who have the critical distance of several years now to reflect on the lessons of this humanitarian intervention must not overlook the good that came of this complicated famine relief effort. Drawing appropriate lessons about the use of necessary force depends on considering all aspects and outcomes of past operations. Intervening on behalf of the population of failed states does not by itself guarantee the desired stability, progress, democracy, economic growth, and humane social standards of development, but a good-faith effort to bring our resources to bear against instability, authoritarian dictatorships, and the continuation of protracted conflict in hot spots around the world demonstrates generosity and moral seriousness. With so much of the world facing political and economic instability (particularly the nations of the former Communist bloc, the Middle East, Africa, and southern Asia), these issues surrounding the legitimacy of nation-building efforts and humanitarian intervention will surely be revisited in coming years. The rebuilding of Iraq after the 2003 conflict is a paradigmatic case of the necessity of expending massive resources in nation-building efforts. The Clinton and Powell doctrines may serve us well by reminding us of prudent limits, but they represent only one part of a socially responsible stance toward a fractured world.

# 6

## ✝

# Recent Christian Approaches to Peacemaking

### RELIGIOUS LEADERS AND FOREIGN POLICY

In recent decades, religious leaders have increasingly engaged in public policy advocacy, speaking on behalf of their denominations or congregations. Usually these forays into public theology involve humanitarian impulses, such as encouraging debt relief to heavily indebted poor nations, or the avoidance of military conflict in favor of diplomatic solutions. Unfortunately, the candid opinion of secular-minded foreign policy elites is that the messages of these "do-gooders" is generally so diffuse, naive, and predictable that they deserve to receive at most a polite but generally not terribly serious hearing in the corridors of power in Congress, the White House, and the State Department.

But there are exceptions to this general rule: religious voices who do their homework and earn the rapt attention of policy-makers. On many of the foreign policy issues surveyed in chapter 5, an irreplaceable role was played by theologians and religious ethicists who attempted to clearly and firmly support moral obligations and questions of social responsibility that surfaced in international crises. None was more thoughtful and forthright than Rev. J. Bryan Hehir, already mentioned in previous chapters as the lead drafter of *The Challenge of Peace*. During the 1980s, he served the U.S. Catholic bishops' conference as head of its Department of Social and Political Affairs. During most of the 1990s, he was professor of the Practice of Religion and Society at Harvard, and later dean of Harvard Divinity School. In 2001, he was named president of Catholic Charities USA.

In numerous articles in religious and secular policy journals, in un-
countable public lectures and papers delivered at meetings of professional societies, Hehir contributed to the debates on just war principles
and their applications sketched previously. Drawing most often from the
tradition of Catholic social teachings, Hehir demonstrated that rare ability to mine a tradition of reflection for its key insights and present them
to a wide audience in a clear and compelling way. Hehir generally relied
on the just war tradition, but neither glossed over difficulties within that
inheritance nor shied away from acknowledging the immense complexity
of applying it to contemporary military contexts, situations that could not
have been anticipated by previous generations of thinkers. He staked out a
nuanced position on expanding the justifications for humanitarian interventions and relativizing the heretofore inviolable principle of national sovereignty.[1] In numerous articles in the religious press, including *America* and
*Commonweal* magazines (besides his often unacknowledged behind-the-
scenes work in ghostwriting many pastoral letters, position papers, and
addresses for the U.S. bishops), Hehir served as the most respected scholarly spokesperson for the Catholic community in the United States regarding issues of war and peace.

Another prominent Catholic scholar of foreign policy is Drew Christiansen, S.J. He also worked extensively with the U.S. bishops, serving
during much of the 1990s as director of the United States Catholic Conference's Office of International Justice and Peace, with particular involvement in Middle Eastern affairs. Among his most impressive publications is an especially well-argued article titled "What We Must Learn
From Kosovo: Military Intervention and Humanitarian Aid." This insightful analysis appeared just weeks after the summer 1999 NATO intervention in Kosovo.[2] In this essay, Christiansen suggested a series of four
institutional reforms in the international community that would assist
constructive interventions in coming decades: (1) various suggestions for the
reform of international law, (2) expansion of nonviolent alternatives to the use
of force, (3) civilian immunity and a risk-averse military, and (4) the eclipse
of military honor and accountability for crimes of air warfare. In perhaps
the most practical piece of wisdom Christiansen shared here, he intro-
duced a crucial distinction in the way contemporary air wars are fought.
Any responsible analysis must insist on distinguishing between "smart
weapons" that are able to surgically degrade an enemy's military capacity, on the one hand, and less precisely targeted weapons that attack infrastructure and tend to degrade the quality of civilian life, on the other
hand. Future judgments regarding the permissibility of warfare must consider the "how" of war-making, beyond merely the questions of
"whether" and "under what circumstances" force may be deployed. Ethical judgments about warfare, even those made by religious voices stray-

ing far from their accustomed areas of expertise, must be informed by these rather technical considerations regarding the technology of contemporary weaponry. Such careful treatments of detailed issues of modern warfare, always held up against the light of the gospel message, represent the best of what the Christian scholarly community brings to the table.

The influence (if not the actual pens) of Hehir and Christiansen is evident in the U.S. Catholic bishops' 1993 statement "The Harvest of Justice Is Sown in Peace."[3] Published as a brief tenth-anniversary reflection to follow up their major pastoral letter *The Challenge of Peace*, this document combines in a particularly rich way two key elements. The first is the hard-headed analysis that must inform religious contributions to foreign policy. The second is an inspiring call to develop a spirituality of peacemaking that includes virtues such as human solidarity and strategies of nonviolent resistance to evil. Particularly impressive is the vehement way the text urges that the cause of peace be reflected constantly in liturgical prayers of petition, preaching, and Catholic education and catechesis. The link between lifestyles of peacemaking and policies of peace has never been drawn as eloquently in any official Catholic document as it is in this reflection. This document sets an agenda that begins with the inner work of "disarming our hearts" and offers resources for this journey of spiritual development. It then proceeds to urge further progress toward nuclear disarmament and the building of institutions that will foster peace in the twenty-first century. That the bishops' advice goes far beyond pious appeals to lofty ideals is amply demonstrated by the list of five well-chosen goals that appear in the middle section of this document: (1) strengthening global institutions, (2) securing human rights, (3) promoting human development, (4) restraining nationalism and eliminating religious violence, and (5) building cooperative security. The bishops earned much praise for supplementing their portrayal of the perfection of peace at the end of time with a rich treatment of interim strategies that will be effective in fostering more proximate improvements that may come to pass in our lifetimes.

## PEACE ACTIVISM AND SCHOLARSHIP

Most of the thinkers and perspectives mentioned in the previous chapters and paragraphs fall within the ambit of the just war tradition of reflection. As such, they labor to encourage the most well-informed judgments possible regarding the use of force for presumably laudable purposes such as national self-defense and humanitarian intervention. By contrast, another group of thinkers influential during recent decades identifies themselves first and foremost as peacemakers and often as practitioners of pacifism, nonviolence, noncooperation with evil, or noncoercive resistance to violence. Instead of focusing primarily on the developments to which foreign policy must respond, they have witnessed with increasing influence and eloquence to the urgency of the gospel mandate to cause no harm to our neighbors, even in dangerous times like the present era.

Over the past twenty years, the religious peace movement has continued to exert a growing influence on public debate. Daniel Berrigan, the Jesuit whose name became a household word over the past few decades, has continued to maintain a high profile, participating in peace actions and writing moving poetry on themes related to peacemaking. Over the past ten years he has published a series of insightful volumes of scriptural commentary on various books of the bible (Job, Lamentations, Jeremiah, Isaiah, Daniel, and Ezekiel) that have inspired him to a life of peace and nonviolence.

Among Berrigan's fellow American Jesuits, perhaps the most impressive younger peacemaker is John Dear, who has written or edited over twenty volumes[4] on themes related to nonviolence and spirituality of peace. His work with organizations such as Plowshares, Pax Christi, and the Fellowship of Reconciliation (the nation's largest and oldest interfaith peace organization, for which he served during the late 1990s as national coordinator) is emblematic of a younger generation of peace activists who were inspired by such early pioneers as Daniel and Philip Berrigan, Eileen Egan, and many members of the Catholic Worker movement. Dear spent many months in prison or under home confinement for participating in acts of civil disobedience and nonviolent resistance, some performed in provocative ways on military bases. As a vivid witness to the profound link between the goals of peace and justice, he has also lived among and worked closely with the poor in their struggle for justice, in places such as inner-city Richmond, rural North Carolina, northern New Mexico, and marginalized neighborhoods of Washington, D.C.

The premier Catholic peace organization in America continues to be Pax Christi USA, part of a worldwide network (Pax Christi International) of Catholics dedicated to peacemaking. It is headquartered in a modest building in Erie, Pennsylvania, and offers an outstanding quarterly publication, *Catholic Peace Voice*. Pax Christi's statement of purpose affirms that it seeks to witness to Christian nonviolence by "rejecting war, preparations for war, and every form of violence and domination. It advocates primacy of conscience, economic and social justice, and respect for creation." Although primarily a lay organization in membership and leadership, Pax Christi USA has been blessed with dozens of members who are bishops, most notably peace activists Walter Sullivan and Thomas Gumbleton.

Much peace activism in recent years has naturally centered around specific issues, some of them focused on embattled regions of the world, such as Israel–Palestine and Iraq, and others on discrete topics worthy of concern, such as efforts against torture, specific weapon systems, and excessive defense spending. An outstanding example is the International Campaign to Ban Landmines, an effective organization whose coordinator Jody Williams was awarded the 1997 Nobel Peace Prize. The annual mid-November demonstration at Fort Benning, Georgia, draws tens of thousands who oppose militarism and human rights atrocities. This Army base is home to the School of the Americas, which trained so many murderous Latin American soldiers, including members of the Atlacatl Battalion that killed, among others, six Jesuits at the University of Central America in El Salvador on 16 November 1989. Maryknoll priest Roy Bourgeois founded School of the Americas Watch, which continues its work in consciousness-raising to foster a human rights-based foreign policy even after the U.S. Army took the cosmetic measure of renaming the international training center at Fort Benning the more euphemistic Western Hemisphere Institute for Security Cooperation.[5] In addition, powerful witnesses against the violence of abortion and capital punishment are led by heroic figures such as Sister Helen Prejean, the subject of the major motion picture *Dead Man Walking*, a chilling story based on Prejean's book describing pastoral work with death-row inmates.

Another stalwart of the peace movement is James W. Douglass, founder of the Ground Zero Community in Poulsbo, Washington. Douglass and his community witnessed throughout the 1990s against the "White Train" that transported nuclear warheads across the Western states. They frequently protested against such U.S. nuclear policies as the relentless arms build-up that included the construction of a class of egregiously expensive Trident submarines in Puget Sound shipyards. The most influential of the books Douglass has authored is *The Nonviolent Coming of God*.[6] In this moving volume, Douglass finds in biblical scenarios, especially the actions and context of the life of Jesus, stunning parallels to the challenges contemporary communities face in forging peace amidst glaring divisions. He argues compellingly that, particularly in the present nuclear age, the urgency of peacemaking cannot be understated. The only alternative to the nonviolent coming of God is, literally, the end of the world. As he stated early in this book, "nonviolent transformation and the threat of destruction are concrete alternatives."[7]

While Berrigan, Dear, and Douglass are better known for their peace activism than their writings per se, scholarship on behalf of peace is the primary contribution of a number of other impressive figures. One is John Howard Yoder, a Mennonite who taught social ethics for many years at Notre Dame before his untimely death in 1997. His oft-reprinted classic *The Politics of Jesus*[8] challenges Christians to take seriously the possibilities of nonviolent resistance and a truly messianic ethic modeled closely on the life and choices of Jesus. Just as solidly grounded in Scripture are the writings of Walter Wink, professor of ethics at Auburn Theological Seminary. Wink offers profound insight into the deepest of human values in his numerous volumes on the topic of peace and on a range of related themes (reconciliation, discernment, prayer, and conversion) that constitute a full-fledged spirituality of peacemaking. Another towering figure of peace scholarship is Stanley Hauerwas, whose numerous works are grounded in narrative ethics. This approach to morality challenges Christians to look beyond the Constantinian turn (which disposed church people, in the name of social responsibility, to make dubious accommodations with power structures such as governments) to our deeper heritage in Jesus of Nazareth, who practiced a countercultural brand of nonviolent resistance to evil.

Writing from his own distinctive perspective as a Southern Baptist peacemaker, Glen H. Stassen contributes a new paradigm of what it means to engage in just peacemaking. He offers a series of concrete and practical action steps to foster a just peace that is far more satisfying than any consideration of just war. His book *Just Peacemaking: Transforming Initiatives for Justice and Peace*[9] is thoroughly informed by Stassen's close knowledge of international security issues. This book, as well as the follow-up volume of essays by various authors that Stassen edited (*Just Peacemaking: Ten Practices for Abolishing War*[10]), includes suggestions for institutional reforms and nonviolent direct action to resist war planning and to build mutual understanding and reconciliation around the world. The work of scholars such as these, as well as the generation of promising young scholars (such as Margaret Pfeil and Michael Baxter of Notre Dame University) who are especially committed to peacemaking, further testifies to the constructive role the academy can play in fostering practical reforms in a dangerous world.

## TERRORISM AND ITS AFTERMATH

Needless to say, a wide range of reactions characterized the response of the religious community to the events of 11 September 2001. Once the immediate response of initial shock, mourning the victims, and comforting the survivors was past, reflection fell into a pattern that represented a spectrum of options as described on the following pages.

At one extreme, church-based reflection was not immune to the surge of patriotism that invariably accompanies times of national emergency and lethal threats to national security. Rallying around the American flag was a natural reaction that kicked in when we realized how viciously we had been attacked. This fervor rendered the most vocal advocates of pacifism extremely unpopular, at least in the short run. In the weeks immediately following the terrorist attacks, demands for swift vengeance were more likely to receive a favorable hearing than pleas for patience and measured responses. The slumbering giant of an inward-looking peace time America had been awakened.

A second wave of reaction involved considerable soul-searching about the underlying cause of the terrorist attacks, as Americans wondered how to understand the events and how to prevent future tragedies. Editorials were full of questions such as "Why do they hate us?" and "How may we be more constructively connected to the rest of the world?" The most perceptive voices sought to make crucial distinctions between the motivations of the terrorists and the authentic message of the Islamic faith, of which Osama bin Laden and the Al Qaeda terrorists are hardly representative. Toward this end, much underbrush needed to be cleared away, including centuries of cultural and linguistic misunderstanding around terms such as "jihad" and "crusade" and the roots of what is almost paradoxically referred to as religious violence.[11] To their credit, most Americans soon found themselves groping their way toward personal and collective efforts at articulating a desire for enhanced security based on true justice and cross-cultural understanding, not mere revenge.

After an initial period of several weeks when quick-response media (radio, television, editorials in newspapers, and Internet postings) shed perhaps "more heat than light" on the issue of terrorism, there appeared a series of thoughtful responses on the part of religious and intellectual communities to the reality of terrorism. Five such documents are mentioned here; four of the five were written and released after the 7 October 2001 commencement of Operation Enduring Freedom, a U.S.-led military endeavor that included a campaign of bombing to destroy Al Qaeda bases in Afghanistan and to defeat the Taliban government that harbored them.

First, the U.S. Catholic bishops used the occasion of their annual fall meeting to draft and issue a 14 November 2001 pastoral message titled "Living with Faith and Hope after September 11."[12] The statement is a very moderate and measured response, pastoral in its tone but insisting on the strictest of ethical standards in shaping a military response to confront terrorism. Here the bishops tended to use pairings of terms (such as "resolve and restraint," "courage and compassion") that reflected their even-handed approach to the new challenge America faces in preventing future terrorist attacks. The document was welcomed by those who locate themselves within the just war tradition, within which the bishops' analysis clearly falls. The statement even includes an appendix of selections from previous church documents that treat just war criteria.

A second, much shorter document was noteworthy for how quickly it appeared. Within thirty-six hours of the 11 September 2001 attacks, dozens (and eventually hundreds) of American religious leaders, primarily in mainline Protestant denominations, had signed an Internet-circulated statement titled "Deny Them Their Victory: A Religious Response to Terrorism." Posted on the website of the National Council of Churches and eventually appearing widely elsewhere in print and electronic media, this two-page reflection offered consolation to victims, urged restraint in U.S. antiterrorism policy, and even partook in some soul-searching about American illusions of invulnerability. In a way more prominent than even the longer and subsequent Catholic bishops' message, this statement challenged U.S. foreign policy-makers to break the cycle of violence by seeking and addressing the deeper causes of world conflict, such as the cultural resentments and the huge economic gaps that separate rich and poor nations. This ecumenical statement's call for a "spirituality of reconciliation" complements the more practical appeal on the part of the Catholic bishops for a prudent use of the categories of the just war theory.

A third document that combines the approaches of the two mentioned previously is Pope John Paul II's "Message for 2002 World Day of Peace," released 8 December 2001 in anticipation of the annual 1 January celebration.[13] Like so many of the pope's statements on war and peace throughout the preceding decade, it succeeds in holding many elements of the Christian tradition in creative tension. After heartfelt expressions of condolences seeking to comfort the victims and survivors, shock at the outrageous scale of destruction, and condemnation of violence (with the stirring cry "You shall not kill in God's name!"), John Paul II addressed the immediate issue of the war against terrorism, since military actions against Al Qaeda and the Taliban in Afghanistan had already begun. The pope called for prudent restraint by the United States, but simultaneously upheld nations' rights to self-defense against terrorism, a move that is very much in line with the Catholic tradition's proclivity for respecting national sovereignty. As John Paul had often done before, he invoked the theological theme of the need for forgiveness and reconciliation. He repeated the mantra ("No peace without justice, no justice without forgiveness") of the reconciliation movement enacted by "Truth and Reconciliation" commissions in sharply divided nations such as South Africa and El Salvador, where massive historic injustices require profound healing. Related themes regarding conflict resolution and reconciliation in politics have been addressed in recent years most perceptively by academics such as Donald Shriver[14] and various members of the legal community. These advocates for reconciliation emerged as key proponents of a new paradigm of restorative justice. The growing literature of this movement aspires to replace a narrow and often mean-spirited retributive justice that is not a secure basis for peace with a more holistic approach to addressing injustices and healing the festering wounds of hatred. The ultimate goal of restorative justice is to reestablish the qualities of trust and good will on which authentic human community depends.

In urging conflicting parties to choose the high road of seeking justice and reconciliation rather than mere retaliation and a cycle of revenge, Pope John Paul II continued his personal mission of witnessing to the values of peacemaking. Although, as he has stated on several occasions, the pope himself is not strictly a pacifist in principle, he has been consistently opposed to the use of deadly force when it comes to recommending policy prescriptions during international conflicts, such as in the Gulf War and the crises in the Balkans and East Timor during the 1990s. Most strikingly, the pontiff's messages repeatedly issue sincere pleas for redoubled efforts at inter-religious dialogue, especially with Islam, as he modeled at the 24 January 2002 World Religions' Day of Prayer for Peace encounter at Assisi, Italy. By praying for peace alongside leaders of other faith communities, John Paul II displayed his ardent desire for a world free from the scourges of war and religiously motivated violence.

A fourth document of interest is titled "The War Must Stop." It was signed by seventy leaders of Catholic institutions in the United States, many of them members and even heads of congregations of women and men, religious and various peace, justice, and advocacy organizations. The three-page statement was released 19 December 2001, about a month after the bishops' statement to which it is a firm rejoinder.[15] The signers found the bishops' approach unsatisfactory for many reasons. The U.S. campaign in Afghanistan, an initiative that the bishops implicitly approved, failed to measure up to several of the standards of the just war theory, including the criteria of last resort, proportionality, and noncombatant immunity, particularly when bombing strategies explicitly consider numerous civilian casualties acceptable as "collateral damage."[16] The letter cut more deeply when it invited our bishops and all Catholics to "rethink the 'Just War' tradition and seek a new paradigm for judging questions of war and peace today." The letter closed with an appeal to witness to the Christian virtues of forgiveness and nonviolence, and listed eleven practical points for further action and reflection, many of them expanding the scope of concern to inquire into the deeper root causes of terrorism and world poverty.

Fifth and finally, in early February 2002, a group of sixty intellectuals (mostly professors of philosophy and public policy, or administrators at universities or conservative think tanks) signed and published "What We're Fighting For: A Letter from America."[17] The statement, organized by David Blankenhorn of the Institute for American Values in New York, is a spirited defense of the Bush administration's conduct of the early months of the war on terrorism. Although it conceded (in a passing aside) that the history of American foreign policy is marked by bouts of "arrogance and

jingoism," this document primarily offered a remarkably uncritical celebration of the American way of life. Using just war principles and even
natural law theory, this diverse group of (primarily secular-minded) intellectual leaders justified the war against terrorism as a necessary effort
to protect America itself as well as "to defend those universal principles
of human rights and human dignity that are the best hope for humankind." Its frame of reference might best be described as civil religion,
for it borrowed some of the trappings of religion (its language, authority,
and resources) to lend support to primarily patriotic goals.

In reviewing this and other literature that appeared shortly after 11 September 2001, it is wise to recall the basic definition of terrorism, as being
at root merely a technique, not truly an end in itself. Terrorism is a means
that certain malevolent people use to the end of disrupting some way of
life to which they object. The growing realization in the months after the
terrorist attacks was that the best way to defeat terrorism is to remain true
to the deepest ideals for which America stands, including tolerance, fair-
ness, and due legal process. One implication of this insight seems obvious: the crackdown on civil liberties, by which key personal rights and
constitutionally protected freedoms were abridged in the name of tighter
security, is a tragic mistake. Policy changes that make America look xeno-
phobic, such as unreasonable racial profiling at airports, draconian immigration restrictions,[18] and the extra-legal seizing and suspected torture of
hundreds of detainees in the name of national security, represent a warp-
ing of the American way of life more often than they appear to be strictly
necessary measures to protect it. Whenever security surveillance becomes
excessive, whenever the right to dissent and free expression is compromised, whenever intelligence and security agencies are given carte
blanche, the terrorists have won another victory. They have disrupted the
way of life they hate.

Another implication is that, seen from the widest perspective, bomb-
ings and warfare are simply not a good or effective way to stop terrorism.
As longtime peace activist and scholar Howard Zinn claimed in one of the
first post-September 11 books to treat the ethics of the war on terrorism,[19]
the struggle against terrorism cannot be won simply with bullets. This is
especially the case today because one of the most vital aspects of world
security in the coming decades will be Muslim public opinion, what is
commonly referred to as "the Arab street." While U.S. policy in the Middle East has for decades focused on maintaining friendly relations with
the government elites of nations that supply so much of our imported oil,
what really matters now are the attitudes of the masses of the Muslim
populace, stretching from Morocco to Indonesia and beyond. Will Western actions provoke them to make a "Huntingtonian scenario" come to
pass, turning numerous nations into "Petri dishes for the breeding of ter-

rorists"? Or can they be persuaded to view the West as an ally in their own aspirations for material and spiritual progress? The answers to these questions, and the peace that depends on them, hang in the balance.

## THE IRAQ CONFLICT AND BEYOND:
## ACTIVISM AND CHRISTIAN REFLECTION

A major occasion for renewed peace activism in both Christian and wider circles was the Iraq conflict of 2003. Although the outcome of events was obviously at variance with the hopes of peace advocates, it was not hard to discern a silver lining amidst the dark clouds of that war. In many ways, the peace movement rediscovered its long-dormant voice during the turbulent months of the build-up to war with Iraq. Prominent among the advocates for a peaceful solution to this crisis were members of religious communities, and specifically Christian church leadership, both in America and around the world.

While Bush was lobbying Congress for approval of his plans to use force against Iraq, Bishop Wilton D. Gregory of Belleville, Illinois, president of the U.S. Bishops Conference, released a 17 September 2002 letter urging the United States to "step back from the brink of war" because "a preemptive, unilateral use of force is difficult to justify at this time."[20] At their next plenary meeting two months later, the entire U.S. Conference of Catholic Bishops issued a longer and more detailed statement of concern about the drift toward war. Reviewing the traditional just war criteria and even citing relevant sections of the Catechism of the Catholic Church, the bishops declared: "We continue to find it difficult to justify the resort to war against Iraq, lacking clear and adequate evidence of an imminent attack of a grave nature. . . . [It] would not meet the strict conditions in Catholic teaching for overriding the strong presumption against the use of military force."[21]

The bishops' expression of hope for alternative means to deal with security concerns without full-scale war was repeated in another poignant statement issued by Bishop Gregory on 26 February 2003, as Christians anticipated the imminent season of Lent and as much of the world recoiled in horror at the looming prospect of hostilities in Iraq. By the time Gregory issued the next bishops' statement on Iraq, released 19 March 2003 just hours before the first American cruise missiles struck Baghdad, there was nothing left to say except to express "deep regret that war was not averted," urge the coalition forces "to observe the moral and legal constraints on the conduct of war," and pledge "to work and pray and hope that the war's deadly consequences will be limited and that civilian life will be protected."[22] A significant controversy brewed when, a week into the fighting in Iraq, questions were raised about whether Catholic soldiers could, in good conscience and without incurring mortal sin, fight in this conflict. Given the serious opposition to the war on the part of the magisterium of the Catholic church, it seemed to some that cooperating with the war effort might be ruled utterly out of bounds. A 25 March 2003 letter to Catholics in uniform from Archbishop Edwin F. O'Brien, head of the Catholic Archdiocese for the Military Services, settled the matter by appealing to the complexity of the issues at stake in the Iraq conflict. The morality of the war remains a matter of prudential judgment, the archbishop advised, and each person is responsible in his or her own conscience for justifying an ethical course of action regarding the conduct of the war.[23]

Leadership from the Vatican was equally strong. Pope John Paul II devoted his annual World Day of Peace message, dated 1 January 2003, to a celebration of the fortieth anniversary of Pope John XXIII's encyclical *Pacem in Terris* (Peace on Earth). Within the context of praising the timeless principles of peace contained in that inspiring document, John Paul II urged a recommitment "to build a world of peace on earth" and to "nurture peace by spreading a spirituality and a culture of peace" amidst the divisions that plague our world today.[24] He mentioned the Middle East as a special focus of concern at the present moment. Two weeks later, at his annual exhortation to the diplomatic emissaries to the Vatican, the pope startled many by dispensing with the usual protocol of such addresses. While such speeches usually confine themselves to generalities of diplomatic concern, the pope on this occasion repeatedly mentioned the deepening Iraq crisis by name. He urged all possible efforts to avert fighting in that volatile region, declaring: "No to war! War is not always inevitable. It is always a defeat for humanity. International law, honest dialogue, solidarity between states, the noble exercise of diplomacy: these are methods worthy of individuals and nations in resolving their differences."[25]

Besides speaking eloquently about the imperative of finding a peaceful solution, Vatican officials conducted a remarkable diplomatic campaign to prevent war in the early months of 2003. The pope dispatched several of his top diplomats to plead the case that war is not a morally acceptable way to resolve contemporary problems. Not only would the Holy See refuse to bless such an invasion as a just war, but Vatican activity suggested that the pope harbored concern that an invasion of Iraq would appear to be a war of aggression. This message was expressed repeatedly by papal spokesman Joaquin Navarro-Valls, Archbishop Jean-Louis Tauran (the Vatican's equivalent of a foreign minister), and Archbishop Renato Martino (president of the Pontifical Council for Justice and Peace and former Vatican observer at the United Nations). This strenuous diplomatic press culminated with the extraordinary 5 March 2003 visit of papal envoy Pio

Laghi to the White House. This Italian cardinal, delivering a personal message from the pope to George W. Bush, repeated the admonition that a U.S.-led invasion of Iraq without U.N. approval would be "immoral, illegal, and unjust."[26] The cardinal, a personal friend of the Bush family for decades, enjoyed a cordial reception, but ultimately left the meeting disappointed in his quest to reverse the march toward war.

In the months just before the war, Vatican City itself became a busy venue for diplomat maneuvering. Visitors to the pope included British Prime Minister Tony Blair, German Foreign Minister Joschka Fischer, Iraq's Deputy Prime Minister Tariq Aziz, and United Nations Secretary General Kofi Annan. Remarking on the significance of these high-profile visits to the ailing pope, the *New York Times* noted that "Vatican City serves as a singular stage for the officials who travel there. . . . World leaders who meet with the pope are clearly seeking to cast their concerns and deliberations in a high-minded light."[27] However, even these many words exchanged in high-level summits finally fell short. On 18 March 2003, when the diplomatic endgame to preserve peace proved to be a failure, papal spokesman Joaquin Navarro-Valls issued a chilling one-sentence statement: "Whoever decides that all the peaceful means made available under international law are exhausted assumes grave responsibility before God, his conscience and history."[28]

Many other Christian voices around the world joined their voices to the choir urging a peaceful settlement to the dispute between the United States and Iraq. The official leadership of many American denominations urged President Bush to pull back from the brink of war, including his own United Methodist Church. Other mainline Protestant groups officially opposing the resort to war included the Presbyterian Church, the Evangelical Lutheran Church in America, the American Baptist Church, the Episcopal Church, the Disciples of Christ, and the United Church of Christ. In addition, strong antiwar positions were taken by the Greek Orthodox Archdiocese of America, the traditional peace churches such as the Mennonites and the Quakers, and even some non-Christian religious groups that normally are reluctant to speak on public affairs.[29] Para-church organizations committed to peace such as Pax Christi and Sojourners took out full-page ads in major periodicals to advocate their antiwar positions, as did ad hoc groups such as Religious Leaders for Sensible Priorities[30] and the secular group Common Cause Iraq Initiative.[31]

The byword of war opposition seemed to be "coalition." Many groups in the United States and abroad formed to protest the drift toward war, and most of them found homes within umbrella groups that increased their effectiveness and coordination. The result was an impressive series of massive rallies and peace demonstrations in world capitals throughout autumn 2002 and spring 2003. None was larger than the worldwide protests held on 15 February 2003, when hundreds of thousands of citizens of dozens of nations on every continent rallied to express their opposition to war. Equally impressive was a rolling candlelight vigil held 16 March 2003, as President Bush prepared to give Saddam Hussein his final ultimatum before the shooting would start. At 7 P.M. in each time zone that evening, candles were lit in a show of peacemaking solidarity at eight thousand vigil sites in 140 nations.[32]

Longtime peace advocates, many of them active since the era of Vietnam War protests, marveled at the renewed spirit of this growing third-millennium peace movement. Somewhat surprisingly, one of the most effective new tools turned out to be the Internet. Once distrusted as a likely source of isolation, alienation, passive entertainment, and mindless escapism, electronic communication has proven to be a boon for activists. Nimble use of interactive websites and e-mail list servers allows umbrella groups to coordinate joint actions in ways unimaginable to previous generations. Impromptu rallies, call-ins to Congress, lightning-quick fund-raising—all are made possible through the power of the World Wide Web. These Internet-savvy activists included three national coalitions, each with its own distinctive identity: International Answer, United for Peace and Justice, and Win Without War. Each is an umbrella group representing many other organizations. The first stands for Act Now to Stop War and End Racism. The second includes both Not in Our Name and September 11 Families for Peaceful Tomorrows, poignant reminders of the origins of the conflict with Iraq. The third includes the National Council of Churches and an intriguing group called MoveOn.org. This latter group is a shoestring organization, but it was able to draw upon an impressive e-mail list of two million willing (and often generously contributing) members to circulate an emergency petition against the war. On 10 March 2003, MoveOn.org delivered the petition to the Security Council of the United Nations. Affixed to it was a list of over one million names of war opponents.[33]

The antiwar coalition surprised many with its ability to muster unprecedented support against the use of arms in Iraq. Inevitably, it labored under the weight of divisions of opinion about tactics, strategies, and goals. How confrontational should protests be? How radical or how mainstream can a peace movement afford to be? Perhaps the most impressive aspect of this most recent campaign for peace was the way it resisted the temptation for knee-jerk sloganeering. The words and actions of war protesters demonstrated a sincere and thoughtful grappling with issues of security in our dangerous world. Rejecting an irresponsible utopianism, leaders of the peace movement reflected deeply on the alternatives to war (renewed weapons inspections, more effective sanctions, and enhanced international cooperation for security) and advocated nonmilitary solutions in measured tones. While their conclusions differed from that of the Bush administration and most members of Congress, they communicated an abiding respect for the differences of opinion that continue to exist in American culture, even while they advocated peaceful means of resolving the Iraq crisis and alternatives to preemptive war.

Nevertheless, stopping terrorists and protecting innocent civilian lives are certainly noble goals and, arguably, sometimes a just cause for military action, at least of a defensive nature. Even while it remains unclear to many which course of action is most advisable in the ongoing struggles of our age, the Christian tradition undoubtedly continues to have much to offer the broader society-wide conversation about war and peace. This is especially true when the Christian community is informed and inspired by sound scholarship that explores, unpacks, and renews our traditions and articulates in a modern key the treasures we have inherited. A recent spate of excellent works has contributed to this task. It is noteworthy that the retrieval of a biblically grounded mandate for peacemaking has found rich ways to inspire Catholic and Protestant Christians in an ecumenically inclusive call to responsible discipleship.

In her 1994 volume *Love Your Enemies: Discipleship, Pacifism and Just War Theory*, Boston College ethicist Lisa Sowle Cahill reassessed the entire Christian tradition of reflection on war with an eye toward subjecting to critical reexamination common opinions that are all too often held uncritically as static dogma.[34] Several impressive recent collections of essays have richly documented Cahill's arguments about the need to reappropriate scriptural texts (such as the Sermon on the Mount) as well as the history of Christian reflection in light of the fundamental demand to follow Jesus, the Prince of Peace, with ever-increasing moral seriousness. Among the more prominent of these volumes are *The Love of Enemy and Nonretaliation in the New Testament*, edited by Willard Swartley,[35] and *War and its Discontents: Pacifism and Quietism in the Abrahamic Traditions*, edited by J. Patout Burns.[36] The deep knowledge of the very roots of the Christian tradition fostered by such scholarly studies encourages believers to put our heads as well as our hearts fully into the call to be peacemakers in a new millennium.

# 7

## +

# Peace and War:
# The State of the Question

### THE SIGNS OF THE TIME

One of the many things that the Second Vatican Council called us to do was to look at the question of war with an entirely new attitude. Part of the problem in dealing with this charge is understanding what attitude we should use to reexamine war. In regard to the traditional just war theory, are we to use the categories of nonviolence or pacifism, or must we step beyond both of these and use some other orientation to evaluate war? Part of the tension and problem of the charge of Vatican II is easily discerned by recalling the statements of the different bishops we surveyed in chapter 4. If one looks at the statements by Cardinal Cooke and then Bishop O'Connor, one sees an evaluation of war in our age within the traditional categories of the just war theory. This produces a very traditional analysis of the issues. Data about the military and the reality of nuclear war seem to be squeezed into an extremely narrow framework that could barely accommodate the issues at hand. This orientation also seems to rely inordinately on the use of ecclesiastical and civil authority and always conveys the impression that the wars in which our nation is involved are just wars. In many ways this orientation, by no means unique to the two authors cited, seems to be leading to the same old questions and to the same old answers. They get us nowhere and we remain enmeshed in the bowels of the war machine and in danger of destruction. The traditional orientation of the just war seems to give us no escape or relief from the terror of our times.

Yet the questions raised by the just war theory remain important. The theory has been used with great profit throughout the centuries to analyze the conduct of nations and soldiers within a particular war. The problem today, however, is that our situation has so dramatically changed with the advent of nuclear weapons and now the question of how to respond to terrorists. One must ask, or at least wonder, whether or not the reality of nuclear warfare, terrorism, and the doctrine of preemptive strikes has literally exploded the boundaries of the just war theory so that it can no longer be used in a constructive fashion. We will profit greatly by continuing to use and ask the questions raised by the just war theory. But at a certain point the theory itself breaks down in the presence of the magnitude of many of the problems that we face.

The writings of Matthiesen and Hunthausen, as analyzed in chapter 4, offer suggestions for approaching war in a new way. Whether or not this orientation will prove useful remains to be proven. However, it is important to attend to some of the issues raised by these bishops in their statements as at least evidence of a new kind of thinking about war that may help us escape the legalistic tendencies of the just war theory and a kind of determinism in thinking about national defense and security.

## A Theology of Peace

A new orientation suggests that peace be the beginning premise rather than the conclusion of one's methodology. Instead of seeing peace only as the end product of armed conflict, one must engage in the process of developing a theology of peace so that one may work actively toward establishing structures in society and relationships among people that will help ensure peace. The state of affairs produced by deterrence and the arms race may not be active conflict, at least at the present moment, but one would hardly describe it as a state of peace because of the tensions and anxiety that the structure itself produces both nationally and internationally. Thus a primary part of a shift in attitude or a reevaluation of war would require that we begin with peace as a premise rather than as a conclusion.

## The Moral Problem of Preparing for War

We need to begin thinking of how deterrence strategy or preparation for even a defensive war—or homeland security, for that matter—affects our lives. Rather than looking at proportionality of means and conducting a harm/benefit analysis or evaluating the status of noncombatants, the bishops are beginning to focus on the extreme amounts of radical disruption that even the preparation for war causes. For example, Bishop Matthiesen refers to the destruction of croplands, the uprooting of families, the depletion of the water supply, and the expansion of services to fulfill short-term needs, a situation that leads to long-term disruption of the work force. Such a moral analysis establishes the priorities to determine how we will conduct our national defense. If it is important that we accept the sacrifices and the disruption of our daily lives required for national defense and security, why do we not accept that peacemaking will also require similar sacrifices and disruption of our lives? We need to recognize that this may be a price that we as Christians need to pay for establishing the structures of peace.

## A Theological Means of Evaluating War

We need a theological basis as the new means of evaluating war. Archbishop Hunthausen provides one orientation that helps to ground a theology of peace. As mentioned earlier, he used the Gospel of Mark with its call to renounce self, take up the cross, and follow Jesus as the touchstone of this orientation. According to Hunthausen, in our day we must think of the concrete and practical ways in which we need to take up the cross. He suggested that taking up the cross in Jesus' time meant being willing to die at the hands of political authorities for the truth of the gospel. In our time, he asserted, taking up the cross might require unilateral nuclear disarmament:

> One obvious meaning of the cross is unilateral disarmament. Jesus' acceptance of the cross rather than the sword raised in his defense is the Gospel's statement of unilateral disarmament. We are called to follow. Our security as people of faith lies not in demonic weapons which threaten all life on earth. Our security is in a loving, caring God. We must dismantle our weapons of terror and place our reliance on God.[1]

While there will be legitimate disagreement on that specific interpretation of the cross in our age, Hunthausen correctly required that we begin translating specific elements of the gospel message that stands behind traditional Christianity into ways of living that will promote peace. He concluded his statement by saying: "God alone is our salvation, through the acceptance in each of our lives of a non-violent cross-suffering love."[2] By each individual's searching for what that means and by having the Church as an institution committed to looking for that kind of nonviolent love, a way to peace is established as a premise and not as a conclusion.

## War and Christian Values

Another orientation toward thinking about war and peace from a new perspective comes from the late Eileen Egan (1911–2000). A peace activist and cofounder of Pax Christi USA, Egan suggested that war reverses the most basic Christian concepts and values, especially as these relate to the Beatitudes and the corporal works of mercy. She pointed out that during times of war, instead of visiting the sick we dramatically increase the number of sick by shooting and bombing individuals. Instead of feeding the hungry, we defoliate forests and fields to guarantee that people cannot eat. We take acres and acres out of use as productive land so that they can be used as battlefields. Instead of burying the dead, we bomb cemeteries.

Many will chalk these regrettable actions up to the unalterable nature of war, but Egan's response must be taken seriously: as Christians, we simply do not engage in such behaviors or allow them to proceed in our name as citizens. We have other values that are more important. We are following another vision, and that vision prohibits us from contradicting our deepest values and virtues that are important to us. When we realize that participation in war makes us act in ways that are utterly inappropriate, that would produce cries of horror in other circumstances, and that also basically contradict our Christian virtues, then we might see war from a different perspective and recognize that it serves to destroy not only life but also the qualities that make life important.

## THE STATE OF THE QUESTION

This section will present several observations regarding how the issue of war and especially the theory of the just war doctrine are being discussed today.

### Problems with the Concept of the Just War

One problem with the just war theory is that war is no longer as contained an enterprise with relatively reversible consequences. In the past, wars had been limited fairly strictly to the territories of the belligerent nations, and even though the effects of the war continued in the wounded veterans, retirement benefits, displaced families, and payments of loans for the conducting of the war, such effects were essentially finite. Such is not the case with nuclear war. Once a high level of radioactivity is released into the atmosphere, its effects will endure for years and the health and ecological consequences of this will be unimaginably destructive. War can no longer be limited, and its effects cannot be reversed.

Traditionally, war has been waged only between a few nations. Even though recent major wars were described as world wars, still only relatively few nations were involved. This situation will also change in the event of a nuclear war. Although only two or three nations may actually deploy nuclear weapons, the entire world will be involved and its fate will be at stake because of the dangers from radioactive fallout. While it was possible in the past to think of war affecting primarily only those nations who were waging it, this approach is no longer viable because of the consequences of nuclear war.

Third, many people are beginning to raise serious objections to the disproportionate amount of money that must be allocated to the military to continue building and deploying ever more lethal weapon systems and to maintain the "appropriate" levels of technology in weaponry, even after the end of the Cold War. The problem is not so much allocating money for the defense of the nation; the problem is a genuine mortgaging, through an increased government debt, of the social well-being of the nation so that more and more armaments may be built. Many people have already experienced serious disruptions in their lives because of the transfer of funds from social programs for health, education, and the relief of poverty to the defense budget. These increases are projected for many years to come and will continue to cause serious problems. Given this set of priorities for defense spending, we may find ourselves in the ironic situation of being the best-defended nation in the world but having little worth defending because the quality of life has utterly disappeared.

## The Critique of the Just War Theory

Serious questions are also being raised about the theoretical structure by which wars are evaluated. In addition to questioning the viability of war itself, the theory by which war has traditionally been justified within Catholicism is also undergoing critique.

### *The Right to Conduct War* (Jus ad bellum)

One of the major problems with the just war theory has to do with the circumstances under which a nation declares war. There is no disinterested worldwide authority to adjudicate among the different nations so that one can know whether a right or an interest is being violated. International politics are presently so complex that it is difficult to disentangle the interests of one nation from another, and the rights of one nation cannot be seen apart from the similar rights of other nations. Terrorism confounds this because one person's terrorist may well be another's freedom fighter. Also, does one include acts of statecraft such as economic boycotts or sanctions as terrorist acts? This situation is even more unclear than before.

A second problem with the right to declare war comes from the traditional postulate that the war must be declared by a competent authority. If a nuclear war was to begin or if a nation was to initiate a first strike, there may be no time to consult with the traditional center of authority within the government. In our country this means the Congress. If the United States was the subject of a nuclear attack, we would only have a few moments to decide whether or not to retaliate, and Congress clearly could not be consulted. If we wished to initiate a first strike, consulting Congress to obtain its authority to declare war would take away all of the advantages of a first strike, namely, the element of surprise. Thus war would be declared either as a consequence of seeing another country's weapons approaching or to gain the advantages connected with a first strike. In the 2003 war with Iraq, the Bush Doctrine of preemptive strike was implicitly validated by Congress when in October 2002 it authorized the used of force against Iraq. However, this doctrine of preemptive strike seriously challenges the traditional interpretation of the just war. Additionally, how does one actually declare war against a terrorist group? These are typically not sovereign nations, but loosely organized cells that operate in semi-autonomy. Is war the correct description for the response to these groups, or would criminal activity be a more accurate description?

Third, another traditional criterion is that victory must be a reasonable prospect. This criterion has undergone the most serious critique because in the event of a nuclear war there is no victory for anyone since the whole world will eventually be compromised from radioactive fallout. If one side in a war uses a nuclear weapon, another side is highly unlikely to exercise restraint but will more than likely respond at least in kind. Once the nuclear exchange begins there can be no victory; there can only be the ashes of defeat, the destruction of the entire planet through radioactive fallout. And in the case of actions against terrorists, how does one know when victory is achieved? When the terrorists are killed or captured or when many of the conditions that gave rise to such violent responses are sufficiently mitigated?

## Duties in the Conducting of War (Jus in bello)

Many problems occur when one considers the traditional moral rules for the conducting of war. How, for example, does one speak of proportionality with radioactivity? There really is no proportionate dose of radioactivity, especially when one takes into account the levels of radioactivity that nuclear weapons will release into the ecosphere.

How can one speak of the immunity of noncombatants when the radioactivity will be released into the atmosphere and distribute itself all over the earth, falling on those who may not even know that a war has begun? Radioactive fallout is not selective in terms of how it falls to the earth. Thus no one—no matter what he or she believes, knows, or feels about a war that has begun elsewhere—enjoys any immunity from falling victim to this kind of warfare.

And in terrorist actions, the primary targets tragically are civilians. The traditionally inviolable rule of the protection of civilian populations in the conduct of war seems to have simply vanished. The strategy of suicide bombing, for example, does not even pretend to be directed at military targets. The purpose is to terrorize the civilian population by killing as many civilians as possible.

A final issue with respect to the traditional criteria for evaluating duties in the conducting of war is that primary targets are not exclusively or primarily military targets—they are cities or civilians. Even though one can argue that many nuclear installations are in close proximity to major urban areas, therefore making urban areas legitimate targets, this still does not take away the reality that part of a strategy of nuclear deterrence and nuclear war is to cause unacceptable levels of civilian casualties on a particular nation. Thus one of the traditional rules of the conduct of war is violated by making all of the citizens of a country hostage to the threat of destruction in a nuclear exchange or by large-scale terrorist activities.

These dimensions of how war is conducted in a nuclear age and an age of increasing terrorist activity make it exceedingly difficult to speak of a just war in the traditional sense. While some would argue that the traditional concepts may still find legitimate application, many more are arguing that such an application is exceedingly more difficult to justify. Others, of course, argue that these points clearly demonstrate that the traditional theory of the just war is utterly useless.

## A NEW DIRECTION

This section will propose key considerations for a new evaluation of war. While the following comments are not a new just war theory, they are ethical concerns that emerge out of contemporary discussions of war and peace and will form part of a new synthesis. At best, the just war theory is under radical critique, and attempts to use it to justify nuclear war are meeting strong resistance. At worst, the theory has been proven to be inapplicable in today's society and consequently we are left adrift and do not have the elements that need to be taken into account as we work through a new synthesis.

### Perceptions of War

*War as an International Event*

War in today's society, especially nuclear war but also conventional war or terrorist activity, will at some point involve the majority of the nations of the world. No one will be able to escape taking sides, and all will be affected in terms of the diversion of resources to the warring nations or preparations for homeland security. In the worst scenario, all will suffer the ravages of radioactive fallout from a nuclear exchange or be hostages to similar threats from terrorists. In our contemporary situation, all the peoples of the earth will equally be victims of war. The land itself will be a victim because, having become radioactive or contaminated with biological agents, it will no longer be fruitful. It is in the interest of all nations to attempt to protect each other, their citizens, and the land and ecosphere that give us life and nourishment. If we do not do this all may be lost.

## The Cost of War

As mentioned above, war is becoming more expensive. This cost is not exclusively financial. More and more of our brightest scientists and engineers are using their talents for the production of weapons of destruction rather than for the development of technologies that will serve life. Not only our money but also our talent, our energy, and our creative thought serve war rather than life. The Reagan administration in particular put a higher priority on the military than on the human services that make life worth living, though that administration was by no means unique. The major ethical problem is examining the priorities of our country and learning what those priorities say about us as a people. What will there be to defend if our nation is turned into a huge armed camp?

We also need to consider our obligations to other nations, particularly those not nearly as fortunate as ours. While each nation ultimately bears the responsibility for its economy and the status of its citizens, nonetheless we are all interconnected. Fostering the improvement of economic and social conditions around the world will help diminish the conditions of deprivation and frustration that are the seeds from which terrorism grows.

## The Consequences of Nuclear War

The enormous consequences that will occur if there is a nuclear exchange have been alluded to several times. And even though the dreaded possibility has been dramatically reduced in the last few years, nuclear arms are still a menace. Many nations as well as terrorist groups seem to want them. Thus the risk of a nuclear exchange remains. High levels of radioactivity will guarantee that there will be few immediate survivors of the nuclear exchange, and the continued presence of radioactivity in the environment will guarantee that the people who survived the first exchange will eventually die hideous deaths because of various illnesses.

Those who survive may be the most unfortunate of all because they are guaranteed an extremely painful death. It is this reality that we must squarely face because there is a fair amount of argumentation that a nuclear war can be survivable. One must look at the consequences of a nuclear exchange and realize that in the long run there can be no survivors. A nuclear exchange will wipe out all of the physical and social structures that are necessary for human life to survive. Even for those individuals who survive the initial exchange, there will be no place to go and no one to care for them. There will be no food, shelter, or energy. Life as we know it will vanish, and in a relatively short time the survivors will also vanish because they will not be able to withstand the ravages of the continued presence of radioactive materials in the environment.

And while the possibility of massive nuclear war seems to be reduced, we still live with the reality of stockpiled nuclear weapons, an underground market in these weapons, and more countries starting up nuclear industries to develop their own weapons. The use of small nuclear weapons as a means of terrorism is also a frightening prospect. The focus has shifted, but the nuclear reality lives on as the legacy of an earlier age.

## Methods of Analysis

### Prophetic

One of the clear orientations emerging out of many contemporary Catholic discussions of war and peace is a prophetic stance against the priorities of our country with respect to both national defense and its cost. More and more bishops are recalling that a very important tradition within Christianity is the tradition of nonviolence, the moral imperative of loving one's enemies. Connected with this we may also refer to the tradition of the suffering servant who bears the burdens of the nation so that the nation may live and prosper.

Instead of focusing on the specific strategic and defense-oriented concepts that have been so much a part of the just war theory, the new prophetic orientation focuses critically on what kind of people we will become if we continue to act the way we have been. This question is extremely important because it involves an examination of our priorities and of the kind of society we wish to have, but it is particularly difficult when applied to issues of international responsibility for widespread poverty, starvation, and unemployment. While it is clear that terrorists have their own agenda, this agenda frequently finds resonance among the poor and marginalized. Such questions ought to be at the heart of the moral analysis of war from a Christian perspective because of the vocation to which we have been called and because of the model provided for us by Jesus.

*Analytic*

In addition to the prophetic dimension there is also a substantive analytic orientation being developed to examine the question of the morality of war in our day. However, this orientation does not approach the question from the same stance as the traditional just war theory. Rather, this analytic orientation looks at the cost of war and the consequences of war in terms of the psychological, physical, and resource dimensions.

We need to ask what will become of us if we continue to invest greater and greater resources into preparations for war. Many are asking whether it is appropriate to mortgage the future of our youth as well as the security of our older citizens for the monies needed to prepare for war. The resource allocation question is becoming much more critical because it is apparent that our resources are finite and we cannot continue to squander them. We currently see the rerouting of enormous funds to antiterrorist activities and homeland defense. And rightly so because citizens need protection. Yet the cost of this comes at a high price, particularly when coupled with the impact of the recession that began in 2001. In such cyclical economic downturns, unemployment increases and benefits become scarce, particularly for those already at the margins of society. Difficult decisions clearly must be made, but there must also be protection for the marginalized, both here and abroad.

Psychologically, we need to attend to what we will become if we continue to live under the specter of the imminent threat of total annihilation or terrorist attack. While these threats may not be as apparent a problem as the issue of resource allocations, nonetheless the issue is important because it produces a wearing down of the spirit, a background condition of numbness that can only lead to the psychological debilitation of everyone. The resource problem also feeds into this psychological dimension because a continued decrease in resources leads to a fear of scarcity, to a selfishness of spirit that puts one's own interests above the common good. Such an orientation works counter to the American tradition of focusing on the needs of others and being concerned about the well-being of our neighbors. The aftermath of 11 September 2001 clearly cast a long and dark shadow of fear across America and caused us to look at one another in new ways. The reality of racial profiling, as well as increased losses of privacy and civil rights, is becoming a more prominent concern. In the short term, such costs can be written off as patriotic sacrifice, but as they become long-term realities, we may experience a genuine wearing down of our spirit and a loss of the very freedom that is the justification for such restrictions.

There is also the problem of the actual financial cost of war itself. Frequently revised cost projections are cause for alarm. These figures range into the trillions of dollars over the next five years to support military operations. It is quite accurate to say that a substantial amount of the budgetary projections for the military involves both the paying of health and retirement benefits and other associated costs to veterans and the maintaining of the armaments that we already have. Nonetheless large amounts of money are being spent for the development of new weapons of destruction as well as for the reestablishment of a biological and chemical warfare potential. It is clear that the budgetary allocations for the military are growing at a rapid rate while the money available for entitlement programs and for social needs is used to pay for war. The ultimate irony of continued spending for the military and decreased spending for social welfare would be the emergence of America as an inviolable fortress but one with nothing but internal decay to protect. The same will be true if valuable social capital is used up to defend curtailments of a variety of freedoms—speech, *habeus corpus*, and privacy—and the subtle reintroduction of racism into our policing policies. Our very restriction of freedom in the name of defending freedom may spell, ironically, a victory for terrorists.

This analytic method of evaluating war focuses on issues that traditionally have not been brought into the just war theory. Rather, it looks more toward the actual costs of preparing for war and what that will do to us as a nation both culturally and individually. Attention to issues such as these sheds new light on preparation for war and how it is waged. It gives us a new lens through which to see the reality of warfare.

## TO WALK IN THE WAY OF PEACE

One of the critical elements in this new orientation is the proposing of a theology of peace. We suggest four qualities that must be part of that orientation, although they are by no means exhaustive.

### A Spirit of Internationalism

One quality we need to develop among all people is a spirit of internationalism. From a practical point of view, internationalism is already a reality because we are all mutually dependent on each other to care for and preserve the goods of this world. We are all bound to our planet by the workings of a delicate ecosystem, and the only way to preserve our resources and ourselves is to look to the good of all.

From a theological point of view, a spirit of internationalism is a very deep part of Christianity. Christianity, along with other religions, proclaims that God is the God of all. Since all are created in the image of God, all are equally brothers and sisters. Such an orientation leads very naturally to a spirit of concern for each other and to a way of seeing one another that can transcend race and nationalism.

## A Spirit of Trust

Trust is a quality that is hard to develop because typically it must be earned rather than presumed. Yet, again, if we are to survive we must begin practicing the kinds of relationships that will lead to trust, and we must begin to work with each other in the expectation that we all are trustworthy. Such an attitude is related to the spirit of internationalism and is based on the reality that our common good is at stake. What we must do is begin engaging in actions that will promote the common good and that will lead us to know that we can indeed work with and trust each other.

## A Spirit of Freedom

One of the most valued qualities of human life, culturally, politically, and religiously, is a spirit of freedom. This spirit allows each human individual to flourish by giving that individual the opportunity to bring forth what is best in himself or herself so that these gifts can be shared with the community. From a political perspective, freedom provides the social structures that allow and encourage all members of a society to promote the freedom of each other and to respect what is brought forth as what is best in the individual.

From the Christian perspective, the truest freedom we have comes from the release from sin and allows us to walk in trust and joy with those we meet along our way. It is also important to remember from a religious perspective that freedom is not only a freedom from sin but also a freedom for action, a freedom for developing those qualities of life that can enhance us and bring out the best in us.

## A Spirit of Love

The gift of love is, from a Christian perspective, the most unique and precious gift that God has given to us, most especially revealed in the gift of Jesus. In his life, Jesus revealed a tremendous love, openness, and acceptance of the men and women that he met. It is this tradition that he has handed on to us, a tradition that he acted out by healing the sick, sharing meals with sinners, washing the feet of his disciples, and accepting death as a means of saving the world.

Such an example of love calls us to respond in a similar way in our own lives. These examples tell us that suffering is a part of love, that efforts must be made to encourage and bring about a spirit of love, and that the offering of love is frequently a gift that is refused. Yet the deepest instinct of Christianity is to ask that this gift continue to be offered and to be put into practice in all the actions of our lives.

The vocation of love that is given to us as Christians is best summed up in the prayer that Saint Francis left us. It is both a prayer and a plan for peace.

Lord, make me an instrument of your peace.
Where there is hatred, let me sow love;
Where there is injury, pardon;
Where there is doubt, faith;
Where there is despair, hope;
Where there is darkness, light;
Where there is sadness, joy.

O Divine Master, grant that I may seek not so much
To be consoled as to console;
To be understood as to understand;
To be loved as to love;
For it is in giving that we receive;
It is in pardoning that we are pardoned;
And it is in dying that we are born to eternal life.

# Notes

## NOTES FOR CHAPTER 1

1. A good survey of the issue of war and peace in world religions, on which some of the following material is based, is John Ferguson, *War and Peace in the World Religions* (New York: Oxford University Press, 1978).

2. For an extended treatment, see Roland Bainton, *Christian Attitudes Towards War and Peace* (New York: Abingdon, 1960).

3. Ibid., pp. 67–8.

4. St. Augustine, *The City of God*, trans. Henry Bettenson (New York: Pelican Books, 1972): Book 19, Chapter 17.

5. St. Thomas Aquinas, *Summa Theologica* 2a–2ae, XI, 1, in *Saint Thomas Aquinas: Philosophical Texts*, ed. Thomas Gilby (New York: Oxford University Press, 1960), p. 348.

6. Francisco de Vitoria, *De Jure Belli*, in "A Historical Perspective on Selective Conscientious Objection," in LeRoy Walters, *Journal of the American Academy of Religion* XLI (June 1973): pp. 201–11, at p. 205.

## NOTES FOR CHAPTER 2

1. Francisco de Vitoria, *De Jure Belli*, 467.60, cited in *The Catholic Tradition of the Law of Nations*, The Catholic Association for International Peace (New York: Paulist Press, 1934), p. 106.

2. Francisco Suárez, *De Legibus ac de Deo Legislatore*, Chapter 13, Section 1, Paragraph 7, cited in *The Catholic Tradition of the Law of Nations*, op. cit., p. 108.

3. Material in this section is based on William F. Roemer et al., *The Catholic Church and Peace Efforts*, The Catholic Association for International Peace (New York: Paulist Press, 1934).

4. Pope Pius XII, "Peace Statements of Recent Popes" (Washington: National Catholic Welfare Conference, 1930), p. 6.

5. Ibid.

6. Vincent A.Yzermans, ed., *The Major Addresses of Pope Pius XII*, Volume II (St. Paul, Minn.: North Central Publishing, 1961), p. 37.

7. Pope Pius XII, "Characteristics of the Christian Will for Peace," 1948 Christmas message, in Yzermans, Volume II op. cit., p. 124.

8. Ibid., p. 125.

9. Pope Pius XII, "International Medical Law," in Yzermans, Volume II, p. 262.

10. Pope Pius XII, "Communism and Democracy," 1956 Christmas message, in Yzermans, Volume II, op. cit., p. 225.

11. Pope John XXIII, *Pacem in Terris*, n. 127.

12. Pope Paul VI, *Populorum Progressio*, n. 31.

13. Pope Paul VI, "If You Wish Peace, Defend Life," 1976 World Day of Peace message, *The Pope Speaks* 22 (1977): 42.

14. Pope Paul VI, "Toward A Balance of Trust," 1978 address to the United Nations, *The Pope Speaks* 23 (1978): 278.

15. Pope John Paul II, *Redemptor Hominis*, n. 16.

16. Pope John Paul II, "The Dignity of the Human Person Is the Basis of Justice and Peace," 1979 address to the United Nations, *The Pope Speaks* 24 (1979): 310.

17. Second Vatican Council, *Gaudium et Spes*, n. 80.

18. Ibid.

19. Ibid.

20. Ibid., n. 79.

21. Ibid.

22. Ibid.

23. Ibid.

24. Ibid., n. 78.

25. Ibid., n. 79.

26. "The Holy See and Disarmament," *The Pope Speaks* 22 (1977): 246. Italics in original.

27. Ibid., p. 247. Italics in original.

28. *Human Life in Our Day*, 1968 pastoral letter of the American Bishops, United States Catholic Conference, Chapter 2.

29. Ibid.

30. Ibid.

31. Ibid.

32. *To Live As Christ Jesus*, 1976 pastoral letter of the American Bishops, United States Catholic Conference.

33. "The Gospel of Peace and the Danger of War," A United States Catholic Conference Pamphlet.

34. John Cardinal Krol, testimony for the United States Catholic Conference before the United States Senate Foreign Relations Committee, in "The Nuclear Threat: Reading the Signs of the Times," Office of International Justice and Peace (Washington, D.C.: United States Catholic Conference, 1976), p. 9.

35. Ibid.

36. Ibid., pp. 9–10. Italics in original.

37. Reverend J. Bryan Hehir, testimony for the United States Catholic Conference before the House Committee on Armed Services in FY 81 Appropriations Authorization Act, 14 March 1980 (Washington, D.C.: United States Catholic Conference).

## NOTES FOR CHAPTER 3

1. John Ford, S.J., "The Morality of Obliteration Bombing," *Theological Studies* 5 (September 1944): 267.

2. John Ford, S.J., "Current Moral Theology and Canon Law," *Theological Studies* 2 (December 1941): 551.

3. Ibid., p. 556. Italics in original.

4. John Ford, S.J., "Moral Theology, 1942," *Theological Studies* 3 (December 1942): 586. Italics in original.

5. Ford, "The Morality of Obliteration Bombing," op. cit., p. 267.

6. Ibid., p. 281.

7. Ibid., p. 291.

8. Ibid., p. 291.

9. Ibid., p. 294.

10. Ibid., p. 302.

11. Ibid., p. 309.

12. Gerald Kelly, S.J., "Notes on Moral Theology, 1950," *Theological Studies* 12 (March 1951): 58.

13. Gerald Kelly, S.J., "Notes on Moral Theology, 1951," *Theological Studies* 13 (December 1952): 66.

14. John C. Murray, S.J., *We Hold These Truths* (Garden City, N.Y.: Image, 1964), p. 244.

15. Ibid., pp. 249–50.

16. Ibid., p. 258.

17. John C. Murray, S.J., "Conscience and the Just War," A Catholic Peace Fellowship booklet.

18. Murray, *We Hold These Truths*, op. cit., p. 255.

19. Paul Hanley Furfey, *The Mystery of Iniquity* (Milwaukee: Bruce Publishing Company, 1944), p. 152.

20. Paul Hanley Furfey, *The Morality Gap* (New York: Macmillan, 1962), p. 73.

21. Ibid., p. 30.

22. Furfey, *The Mystery of Iniquity*, op. cit, p. 161.

23. Furfey, *The Morality Gap*, op. cit., p. 139.

24. Ibid.

25. Patricia McNeal, *The American Catholic Peace Movement: 1928–1972* (New York: Arno Press, 1978), pp. 64–78.

26. William Miller, *A Harsh and Dreadful Love* (New York: Liveright, 1973), p. 160.

27. Gordon C. Zahn, ed., *The Nonviolent Alternative* (New York: Farrar, Straus and Giroux, 1980), p. 67.

28. Ibid., p. 68.

29. Ibid., pp. 34–5.

30. Ibid., p. 88.

31. Ibid., p. 89.

32. Ibid., p. 85.

33. Ibid., p. 161. Italics in original.

34. Daniel Berrigan, S.J., *The Bride* (New York: Macmillan, 1959).

35. Daniel Berrigan, S.J., *No Bars to Manhood* (Garden City, N.Y: Doubleday, 1970), p. 107.

36. Daniel Berrigan, S.J., *The Trial of the Catonsville Nine* (Boston: Beacon Press, 1970).

37. J. Bryan Hehir, "The Just War Ethic and Catholic Theology: Dynamics of Change and Continuity," in *War or Peace: The Search for New Answers*, ed. Thomas A. Shannon (Maryknoll, N.Y: Orbis Press, 1979), p. 22.

38. Ibid., p. 27.

39. Ibid., p. 32.

40. Charles E. Curran, *Politics, Medicine, and Christian Ethics* (Philadelphia: Fortress Press, 1973), p. 75.

41. Ibid., p. 78.

42. Ibid., p. 99.

43. Charles E. Curran, *American Catholic Social Ethics: Twentieth Century Approaches* (Notre Dame, Ind.: University of Notre Dame Press, 1982).

44. Among Zahn's major contributions are the following: *War Conscience and Dissent* (New York: Hawthorn, 1967), *In Solitary Witness* (Boston: Beacon Press, 1964), and *Another Part of the War: The Camp Simon Story* (Amherst: University of Massachusetts Press, 1979).

## NOTES FOR CHAPTER 4

1. Archbishop Joseph L. Bernardin, "Report of the National Council of Catholic Bishops Ad Hoc Committee on War and Peace" (Washington, D.C.: United States Catholic Conference, 1981).

2. Ibid.

3. Cf. the full text of Bishop Pilla's statement for further development of this idea.

4. Archbishop John R. Quinn, "Instruments of Peace, Weapons of War" (Boston: Daughters of Saint Paul, 1981), p. 10.

5. Ibid., p. 11.

6. Bishop L. T. Matthiesen, Statement on the MX Missile System (presented 20 April 1981), *West Texas Catholic*, 3 May 1991.

7. Bishop L. T. Matthiesen, Statement on the Production and Stockpiling of the Neutron Bomb (presented 23 August 1981), *West Texas Catholic*.

8. Archbishop Raymond G. Hunthausen, "Faith and Disarmament," speech delivered to the Pacific Northwest Synod for the Lutheran Church in America, 12 June 1981.

9. Ibid.

10. Archbishop Raymond G. Hunthausen, speech to peace rally, sponsored by Nuclear Weapons Freeze Committee, 24 October 1981.

11. Ibid.

12. Archbishop Raymond G. Hunthausen, pastoral letter, 28 January 1982.

13. Vatican Council II, *Gaudium et Spes*, n. 79.

14. Terrence Cardinal Cooke, pastoral letter to Catholic chaplains of the armed services, p. 2. Italics in original.

15. Ibid., p. 4.

16. Bishop John J. O'Connor, *In Defense of Life* (Boston: Daughters of Saint Paul, 1981).

17. Ibid., p. 65.

18. Ibid., pp. 28ff.

19. *National Catholic Reporter* 18, no. 34, (2 July 1982) *Commonweal* 109, no. 14, (13 August 1982)

20. *The Challenge of Peace*, # 85–110, in *Catholic Social Thought: The Documentary Heritage*, eds. David J. O'Brien and Thomas A. Shannon (Maryknoll, NY: Orbis Books, 1992). The citations refer to the paragraph numbers.

21. Ibid., # 147.

22. Ibid., # 150.

23. Ibid., # 157. Italics in original.

24. Ibid., # 158.

25. Ibid., # 159.

26. Ibid., # 169.

27. Ibid., # 178.

28. Ibid., # 181.

29. Ibid., # 186.

30. Ibid., # 188.

31. Ibid., # 190.

32. Ibid., # 191.

33. Ibid., # 10.

34. Ibid., # 12.

## NOTES FOR CHAPTER 5

1. Francis Fukuyama, *The End of History and the Last Man* (New York: Free Press, 1992).

2. Samuel P. Huntington, *The Clash of Civilization and the Remaking of World Order* (New York: Touchstone Books, 1996).

3. Ibid., p. 207.

4. Stanley Hoffman, *Duties Beyond Borders: On the Limits and Possibilities of Ethical International Politics* (Syracuse: Syracuse University Press, 1981).

5. See for example Joel H. Rosenblum, ed., *Ethics and International Affairs: A Reader*, 2nd ed. (Washington, D.C.: Georgetown University Press, 1999). This volume contains an essay by Hoffman himself, as well as many of his former students and others indebted to his scholarship.

6. Both these quotes are taken from this bishops' committee's summary document "The Strategic Defense Initiative: Moral Questions, Public Choices." This booklet as well as the longer full text ("A Report on the *Challenge of Peace* and Policy Developments 1983–88") is available from the Office of Publishing and Promotion Services of the USCCB in Washington, D.C.

7. "Resolution That Congress Approved on the Right to Use Force in Iraq," *New York Times*, 12 October 2002, A10.

8. David E. Sanger, "Bush to Outline Doctrine of Striking Foes First," *New York Times*, 20 September 2002, A1.

9. "Changes in Strategy for National Security," *New York Times*, 20 September 2002, A10.

10. Michael Kelly, "A Doctrine of Armed Evangelism," *Washington Post*, 9 October 2002, A31. Tragically, only six months after writing these words, Kelly died when the military vehicle in which he was riding while covering the war in Iraq flipped over and landed in a ditch.

11. Mark Danner, "The Struggles of Democracy and Empire," *New York Times*, 9 October 2002, A31.

12. Jim Hug, S.J., "Our National Security Strategy: Betrayal of the American Spirit," *CenterFocus: News From the Center of Concern*, February–March 2003, pp. 1–3, 14.

13. George Weigel, "The Just War Case for the War," *America*, 31 March 2003, pp. 7–10. Another prominent conservative Catholic, Michael Novak of the American Enterprise Institute, also championed the argument that the preemptive war against Iraq could be justified using traditional just war criteria, even taking his case to Rome in February 2003 to discuss this innovation in just war theory with Vatican officials. See the text of Novak's presentation to a 10 February 2003 Vatican symposium in "An Argument That War Against Iraq Is Just," *Origins* 32, no. 36 (20 February 2003): 593, 595–8.

14. Jimmy Carter, "Just War—Or a Just War?" *New York Times*, 9 March 2003, Section 4, p. 17.

15. Joseph S. Nye, Jr., *The Paradox of American Power: Why the World's Only Superpower Can't Go It Alone* (New York: Oxford University Press, 2002).

16. Samantha Power, *"A Problem from Hell": America and the Age of Genocide* (New York: Basic Books, 2002).

17. Michael Ignatieff, *The Warrior's Honor: Ethnic War and the Modern Conscience* (New York: Owl Books, 1997).

18. Michael Ignatieff, *Human Rights as Politics and Idolatry* (Princeton: Princeton University Press, 2001).

19. Michael Ignatieff, *Virtual War: Kosovo and Beyond* (New York: Picador, 2001).

## NOTES FOR CHAPTER 6

1. See, for example, Hehir's essay "Military Intervention and National Sovereignty: Recasting the Relationship," in *Hard Choices*, ed. Jonathan Moore (Lanham, Md.: Rowman & Littlefield, 1999), pp. 29–54; and his article "Kosovo: A War of Values and the Values of War," *America*, 15 May 1999, pp. 7–12.

2. Christiansen's article appears in *America*, 28 August 1999, pp. 7–10.

3. This statement appears in *Origins* 23, no. 26 (9 December 1993): 449–64.

4. For abundant information about the publications and activities of John Dear, S.J., see the website www.fatherjohndear.org.

5. For information about School of the Americas Watch, see its website www.soaw.org.

6. James W. Douglass, *The Nonviolent Coming of God* (Maryknoll, N.Y.: Orbis Books, 1991).

7. Ibid., p. 3.

8. John Howard Yoder, *The Politics of Jesus*: Vicit Agnus Noster (Grand Rapids, Mich.: William B. Eerdmans Press, 1971).

9. Glen H. Stassen, *Just Peacemaking: Transforming Initiatives for Justice and Peace* (Louisville, Ky.: Westminster/John Knox Press, 1992).

10. Glen H. Stassen, ed., *Just Peacemaking: Ten Practices for Abolishing War* (Cleveland: Pilgrim Press, 1998).

11. Perhaps the best contemporary work on religiously motivated violence is Mark Juergensmeyer, *Terror in the Mind of God: The Global Rise of Religious Violence*, updated edition with a new preface, in the series *Comparative Studies in Religion and Society* (Berkeley, Calif.: University of California Press, 2001). Also highly regarded is R. Scott Appleby, *The Ambivalence of the Sacred: Religion, Violence and Reconciliation* (Lanham, Md.: Rowman & Littlefield, 2000).

12. The full text appears in *Origins* 31, no. 25 (29 November 2001): 413–20. It also appears online at www.usccb.org/sdwp/sept11.htm [accessed 10 August 2002].

13. It appears in *America*, 7 January 2002, pp. 7–11.

14. Donald W. Shriver Jr., *An Ethic for Enemies: Forgiveness in Politics* (New York: Oxford University Press, 1995). See also Gregory Baum and Howard Wells, eds., *The Reconciliation of Peoples: Challenge to the Churches* (Maryknoll, N.Y.: Orbis Books, 1997).

15. The full text appears in *Origins* 31, no. 30 (10 January 2002): 505–7.

16. The letter cites statistics from Dr. Marc Herold of the University of New Hampshire who studied international press reports to document at least 3,767 civilian casualties in the first nine weeks of bombing and fighting in Afghanistan. Other estimates of the civilian toll, a topic that elicited much media attention at the time, varied greatly. Useful links about this issue may be obtained from www.media-alliance.org/mediafile/20-5/index.html [accessed 10 August 2002].

17. "What We're Fighting For: A Letter from America," *The Responsive Community* 12, no. 4 (fall 2002): 30–42.

18. See Robert McChesney, S.J., "Immigration and Terrorism: The Issues Have Become Blurred and Entangled," *America*, 29 October 2001, pp. 8–11.

19. Howard Zinn, *Terrorism and War* (New York: Seven Stories Press, 2002).

20. Bishop Wilton D. Gregory, "Letter to President Bush on the Iraq Situation," *Origins* 32, no. 6 (26 September 2002): 261, 263–4.

21. United States Conference of Catholic Bishops, "Statement on Iraq," *Origins* 32, no. 24 (21 November 2002): 406–8.

22. Bishop Wilton D. Gregory, "On the Brink of War: A Statement," *Origins* 32, no. 41 (27 March 2003): 687–8. See also the account of Bishop Gregory's statement of 19 March 2003 as reported in "Bishops' Conference President on War and Wartime Conduct," *America*, 31 March 2003, pp. 4–5.

23. The full text of this 25 March 2003 letter appears in Archbishop Edwin F. O'Brien, "Carrying Out Military Duties in Good Conscience," *Origins* 32, no. 42 (3 April 2003): 693. For coverage of this issue, see Alan Cooperman, "Prelate Reassures Catholic Soldiers: Service in Iraq War Sanctioned," *Washington Post*, 2 April 2003, A28. On one side of this controversy, Bishop John Michael Botean, prelate of the Romanian Byzantine Catholic Church in America, had issued a stunning 7 March statement. This leader of five thousand faithful in full communion with the Roman Catholic Church had unambiguously called "any direct participation in and support of this war against the people of Iraq [an] objectively grave evil, a matter of mortal sin." The full text of Bishop Botean's appeal appears in "Bishop Declares Iraq War Objectively Evil," *Origins* 32, no. 42 (3 April 2003): 694–5. By mid-March, other Catholic prelates, including Washington's Cardinal Theodore McCarrick, had expressed mediating positions in the controversy. They wished strongly to condemn the decision to start the war without intending to place Catholics in the armed services in the impossible situation of obeying either the orders of their military superiors or the moral admonitions of their bishops. Needless to say, Archbishop O'Brien's pronouncement in favor of freedom of conscience did not settle the matter to the satisfaction of all observers.

24. John Paul II, "*Pacem in Terris*: A Permanent Commitment," *Origins* 32, no. 29 (2 January 2003): 484–7. These quoted words appear in paragraphs 9–10. Although marking the 1 January 2003 celebration of the World Day of Peace, this message was actually released 8 December 2002.

25. The full text of John Paul II's address appears as "The International Situation Today," *Origins* 32, no. 33 (30 January 2003): 543–5. See also Frank Bruni, "Pope Voices Opposition, His Strongest, to Iraq War," *New York Times*, 14 January 2003, A11.

26. "Papal Envoy Meets Bush," *America*, 17 March 2003, p. 4.

27. Frank Bruni, "Threat of War Draws World Leaders, with Different Views, to the Pope's Door," *New York Times*, 22 February 2003, A6.

28. "Vatican: Those Who Give Up on Peace Must Answer to God," *America*, 31 March 2003, p. 5.

29. For a more complete list, see Laurie Goodstein, "Diverse Denominations Oppose the Call to Arms," *New York Times*, 6 March 2003, A12. Excerpts from antiwar statements of many religious groups are contained in "Vatican Laments Start of War," *National Catholic Reporter*, 28 March 2003, p. 3.

30. See their full-page letter addressed directly to President Bush, *New York Times*, 4 December 2002, A33.

31. See their sign-on petition letter objecting to the Bush Doctrine, *New York Times*, 1 October 2002, A21.

32. For details see the editorial column "The Peace Enterprise Goes Global," *National Catholic Reporter*, 28 March 2003, p. 28.

33. For further information about these coalitions, see Kate Zernike and Dean E. Murphy, "Antiwar Effort Emphasizes Civility Over Confrontation," *New York Times*, 29 March 2003, B1, B13.

34. Lisa Sowle Cahill, *Love Your Enemies: Discipleship, Pacifism and Just War Theory* (Minneapolis: Fortress Press, 1994).

35. Willard M. Swartley, ed., *The Love of Enemy and Nonretaliation in the New Testament* (Louisville, Ky.: Westminster/John Knox Press, 1992).

36. J. Patout Burns, *War and its Discontents: Pacifism and Quietism in the Abrahamic Traditions* (Washington, D.C.: Georgetown University Press, 1996).

## NOTES FOR CHAPTER 7

1. Archbishop Raymond G. Hunthausen, pastoral letter, 28 January 1982.
2. Ibid.

# Bibliography

Appleby, R. Scott. *The Ambivalence of the Sacred: Religion, Violence and Reconciliation.* Lanham, Md.: Rowman & Littlefield, 2000.

Aquinas, St. Thomas. *Summa Theologica.* In *Saint Thomas Aquinas: Philosophical Texts,* edited by Thomas Gilby. New York: Oxford University Press, 1960.

Augustine, St. *The City of God.* Trans. Henry Bettenson. New York: Pelican Books, 1972.

Bainton, Roland. *Christian Attitudes Towards War and Peace.* New York: Abingdon, 1960.

Baum, Gregory, and Howard Wells, eds. *The Reconciliation of Peoples: Challenge to the Churches.* Maryknoll, N.Y.: Orbis Books, 1997.

Bernardin, Archbishop Joseph L. "Report of the National Council of Catholic Bishops Ad Hoc Committee on War and Peace." Washington, D.C.: United States Catholic Conference, 1981.

Berrigan, Daniel, S.J. *The Bride.* New York: Macmillan, 1959.

———. *No Bars to Manhood,* Garden City, N.Y.: Doubleday, 1970.

———. *The Trial of the Catonsville Nine.* Boston: Beacon Press, 1970.

"Bishops' Conference President on War and Wartime Conduct." *America,* 31 March 2003, pp. 4–5.

Botean, Bishop John Michael. "Bishop Declares Iraq War Objectively Evil." *Origins* 32, no. 42 (3 April 2003): 694–5.

Bruni, Frank. "Pope Voices Opposition, His Strongest, to Iraq War." *New York Times,* 14 January 2003, A11.

———. "Threat of War Draws World Leaders, with Different Views, to the Pope's Door." *New York Times,* 22 February 2003, A6.

Burns, J. Patout. *War and its Discontents: Pacifism and Quietism in the Abrahamic Traditions.* Washington, D.C.: Georgetown University Press, 1996.

Cahill, Lisa Sowle. *Love Your Enemies: Discipleship, Pacifism and Just War Theory.* Minneapolis: Fortress Press, 1994.

Carter, Jimmy. "Just War—Or a Just War?" *New York Times*, 9 March 2003, Section 4, p. 17.

"Changes in Strategy for National Security." *New York Times*, 20 September 2002, A10.

Christiansen, Drew. "What We Must Learn From Kosovo: Military Intervention and Humanitarian Aid." *America*, 28 August 1999, pp. 7–10.

Cooperman, Alan. "Prelate Reassures Catholic Soldiers: Service in Iraq War Sanctioned." *Washington Post*, 2 April 2003, A28.

Curran, Charles E. *Politics, Medicine, and Christian Ethics*. Philadelphia: Fortress Press, 1973.

——. *American Catholic Social Ethics: Twentieth Century Approaches*. Notre Dame, Ind.: University of Notre Dame Press. 1982.

Danner, Mark. "The Struggles of Democracy and Empire." *New York Times*, 9 October 2002, A31.

Douglass, James W. *The Nonviolent Coming of God*. Maryknoll, N.Y.: Orbis Books, 1991.

Ferguson, John. *War and Peace in the World Religions*. New York: Oxford University Press, 1978.

Ford, John, S.J. "The Morality of Obliteration Bombing." *Theological Studies* 5 (September 1944): 261–309.

Fukuyama, Francis. *The End of History and the Last Man*. New York: Free Press, 1992.

Furfey, Paul Hanley. *The Mystery of Iniquity*. Milwaukee: Bruce Publishing Company, 1944.

——. *The Morality Gap*. New York: Macmillan, 1962.

Goodstein, Laurie. "Diverse Denominations Oppose the Call to Arms." *New York Times*, 6 March 2003, A12.

Gregory, Bishop Wilton D. "Letter to President Bush on the Iraq Situation." *Origins* 32, no. 6 (26 September 2002): 261, 263–4.

——. "On the Brink of War: A Statement." *Origins* 32, no. 41 (27 March 2003): 687–8.

Hehir, J. Bryan. "The Just War Ethic and Catholic Theology: Dynamics of Change and Continuity." In *War or Peace: The Search for New Answers*, edited by Thomas A. Shannon, pp. 15–39 Maryknoll, N.Y: Orbis Press, 1979.

——. Testimony for the United States Catholic Conference before the House Committee on Armed Services in FY 81 Appropriations Authorization Act, 14 March 1980. Washington, D.C.: United States Catholic Conference.

——. "Kosovo: A War of Values and the Values of War." *America*, 15 May 1999, pp. 7–12.

——. "Military Intervention and National Sovereignty: Recasting the Relationship." In *Hard Choices*, edited by Jonathan Moore, pp. 29–54. Lanham, Md.: Rowman & Littlefield, 1999.

Hoffman, Stanley. *Duties Beyond Borders: On the Limits and Possibilities of Ethical International Politics*. Syracuse: Syracuse University Press, 1981.

"The Holy See and Disarmament." *The Pope Speaks* 22 (1977), p. 246.

Hug, Jim, S.J. "Our National Security Strategy: Betrayal of the American Spirit." *CenterFocus: News From the Center of Concern* (February–March 2003), pp. 1–3, 14.

Huntington, Samuel P. *The Clash of Civilization and the Remaking of World Order.* New York: Touchstone Books, 1996.

Ignatieff, Michael. *The Warrior's Honor: Ethnic War and the Modern Conscience.* New York: Owl Books, 1997.

———. *Human Rights as Politics and Idolatry.* Princeton: Princeton University Press, 2001.

———. *Virtual War: Kosovo and Beyond.* New York: Picador, 2001.

Juergensmeyer, Mark. *Terror in the Mind of God: The Global Rise of Religious Violence,* updated edition with a new preface. In the series *Comparative Studies in Religion and Society.* Berkeley, Calif.: University of California Press, 2001.

Kelly, Michael. "A Doctrine of Armed Evangelism." *Washington Post,* 9 October 2002, A31.

McChesney, Robert, S.J. "Immigration and Terrorism: The Issues Have Become Blurred and Entangled." *America,* 29 October 2001, pp. 8–11.

McNeal, Patricia. *The American Catholic Peace Movement: 1928–1972.* New York. Arno Press, 1978.

Miller, William. *A Harsh and Dreadful Love.* New York: Liveright, 1973.

Murray, John C., S.J. *We Hold These Truths.* Garden City, N.Y.: Image, 1964.

Novak, Michael. "An Argument That War Against Iraq Is Just," *Origins* 32, no. 36 (20 February 2003): 593, 595–8.

Nye, Jr., Joseph S. *The Paradox of American Power: Why the World's Only Superpower Can't Go It Alone.* New York: Oxford University Press, 2002.

O'Brien, Archbishop Edwin F. "Carrying Out Military Duties in Good Conscience." *Origins* 32, no 42 (3 April 2003): 693.

O'Connor, Bishop John J. *In Defense of Life.* Boston: Daughters of Saint Paul, 1981.

"Papal Envoy Meets Bush." *America,* 17 March 2003, p. 4.

"The Peace Enterprise Goes Global." *National Catholic Reporter,* 28 March 2003, p. 28.

*Peace Statements of Recent Popes.* Washington, D.C.: National Catholic Welfare Conference, 1930.

Pope John Paul II. "The Dignity of the Human Person Is the Basis of Justice and Peace," 1979 address to the United Nations. *The Pope Speaks* 24 (1979), p. 310.

———. "Message for 2002 World Day of Peace." *America,* 7 January 2002, pp. 7 11.

———. "*Pacem in Terris*: A Permanent Commitment." *Origins* 32, no. 29 (2 January 2003): 484–7.

———. "The International Situation Today." *Origins* 32, no. 33 (30 January 2003): 543–5.

Pope Paul VI, *Populorum Progressio,* 26 March 1967.

———. "If You Wish Peace, Defend Life," 1976 World Day of Peace message. *The Pope Speaks* 22 (1977), p. 42.

———. "Toward A Balance of Trust," 1978 message to the United Nations. *The Pope Speaks* 23 (1978), p. 278.

Power, Samantha. *"A Problem from Hell": America and the Age of Genocide.* New York: Basic Books, 2002.

"Resolution That Congress Approved on the Right to Use Force in Iraq." *New York Times,* 12 October 2002, A10.

Roemer, William F., et al. *The Catholic Church and Peace Efforts,* The Catholic Association for International Peace. New York: Paulist Press, 1934.

Rosenblum, Joel H., ed. *Ethics and International Affairs: A Reader*, 2nd ed. Washington, D.C.: Georgetown University Press, 1999.

Sanger, David E. "Bush to Outline Doctrine of Striking Foes First." *New York Times*, 20 September 2002, A1, A10.

Shriver, Donald W., Jr. *An Ethic for Enemies: Forgiveness in Politics*. New York: Oxford University Press, 1995.

Stassen, Glen H. *Just Peacemaking: Transforming Initiatives for Justice and Peace*. Louisville, Ky.: Westminster/John Knox Press, 1992.

——, ed. *Just Peacemaking: Ten Practices for Abolishing War*. Cleveland: Pilgrim Press, 1998.

Suárez, Francisco. *De Legibus ac de Deo Legislatore*. Ed. Luciano Pereña. Six volumes. Madrid: Consejo Superior de Investigationes Cientificas, 1971.

Swartley, Willard M., ed. *The Love of Enemy and Nonretaliation in the New Testament* Louisville, Ky.: Westminster/John Knox Press, 1992.

United States Catholic Conference of Bishops. *Human Life in Our Day*, 1968.

——. *To Live As Christ Jesus*, 1976.

——. *The Challenge of Peace*, 1983.

——. "The Strategic Defense Initiative: Moral Questions, Public Choices." Washington, D.C.: USCCB Office of Publishing and Promotion Services, 1988.

——. "The Harvest of Justice Is Sown in Peace." *Origins* 23, no. 26 (9 December 1993): 449–64.

——. "Living with Faith and Hope after September 11." *Origins* 31, no. 25 (29 November 2001): 413–20.

——. "Statement on Iraq." *Origins* 32, no. 24 (21 November 2002): 406–8.

"Vatican Laments Start of War." *National Catholic Reporter*, 28 March 2003, p. 3.

"Vatican: Those Who Give Up on Peace Must Answer to God." *America*, 31 March 2003, p. 5.

Vitoria, Francisco de. *De Jure Belli*, 467.60. Quoted from the *Catholic Tradition of the Law of Nations*, The Catholic Association for International Peace. New York: Paulist Press, 1934, p. 106.

Walters, LeRoy. "A Historical Perspective on Selective Conscientious Objection." *Journal of the American Academy of Religion* XLI (June 1973): 201–11.

"The War Must Stop." *Origins* 31, no. 30 (10 January 2002): 505–7.

Weigel, George. "The Just War Case for the War." *America*, 31 March 2003, pp. 7–10.

"What We're Fighting For: A Letter from America." *The Responsive Community* 12, no. 4 (fall 2002): 30–42.

Yoder, John Howard. *The Politics of Jesus*: Vicit Agnus Noster. Grand Rapids, Mich.: William B. Eerdmans Publishing Co., 1971.

Zahn, Gordon C. *In Solitary Witness*. Boston: Beacon Press, 1964.

——. *War, Conscience and Dissent*. New York: Hawthorn, 1967.

——. *Another Part of the War: The Camp Simon Story*. Amherst: University of Massachusetts Press, 1979.

——, ed. *The Nonviolent Alternative*. New York: Farrar, Straus and Giroux, 1980.

Zernike, Kate, and Dean E. Murphy. "Antiwar Effort Emphasizes Civility Over Confrontation." *New York Times*, 29 March 2003, B1, B13.

Zinn, Howard. *Terrorism and War*. New York: Seven Stories Press, 2002.

# Index

# About the Authors

**Thomas Massaro**, S.J. is associate professor of moral theology at Weston Jesuit School of Theology in Cambridge, Massachusetts. He teaches courses in Catholic social ethics and lectures frequently on topics involving the church and social justice. His research addresses the moral evaluation of American policies regarding domestic and international poverty, as well as foreign policy and globalization. He is the author of three previous books, including *Living Justice: Catholic Social Teaching in Action* (Sheed & Ward, 2000).

**Thomas A. Shannon** is professor of religion and social ethics in the Department of Humanities and Ethics at Worcester Polytechnic Institute. He is the author and editor of many books and articles in the areas of social ethics, assisted reproduction, and genetic engineering. He is the coauthor of *The New Genetic Medicine* and the series editor of Readings in Bioethics, both from Sheed and Ward.